ANTIQUES
FOR THE
TABLE

A COMPLETE GUIDE TO DINING ROOM ACCESSORIES
FOR COLLECTING AND ENTERTAINING

ANTIQUES FOR THE TABLE

SHEILA CHEFETZ • PHOTOGRAPHY BY JOSHUA GREENE

TEXT BY ALEXANDRA ENDERS

STYLING BY SUSANNA STRATTON—NORRIS

DESIGN BY SUSAN SLOVER DESIGN

RESEARCH BY SUSAN WILLIAMS

PENGUIN
STUDIO

To the memory of my mother, Ida Rossman...
for whom "being with the family" meant planning events,
parties, and dinners that provided nourishment for her life
and forever enriched mine   —S.C.

To my mother, who loves dinner parties and
entertaining, and my father, whose love of food filled
the plates with surprise   —J.G.

Penguin Studio Books
Published by the Penguin Group
Penguin Books USA Inc., 375 Hudson Street,
New York, New York 10014, U.S.A.
Penguin Books Ltd, 27 Wrights Lane,
London W8 5TZ, England
Penguin Books Australia Ltd, Ringwood,
Victoria, Australia
Penguin Books (N.Z.) Ltd, 182-190 Wairau Road,
Auckland 10, New Zealand

Penguin Books Ltd, Registered Offices:
Harmondsworth, Middlesex, England

First published in 1993 by Viking Penguin,
a division of Penguin Books USA Inc.

10 9 8 7 6 5 4

Library of Congress Cataloging-in-Publication Data
Chefetz, Sheila.
    Antiques for the table : a complete guide to dining-room
    accessories for collecting and entertaining / Sheila Chefetz;
    photographs by Joshua Greene; text by Alexandra Enders.
        p. ca.
    IS8N 0-670-84057-2
    1. Antiques 2. Table setting and decoration-Collectibles.
I. Enders. Alexandra. II. Title.
NK1125.C44 1993
745. 1--ac20   92-50728 CIP

Printed in Hong Kong

CONTENTS

INTRODUCTION

WHEN I WAS A CHILD, OUR DINING ROOM WAS NEITHER LARGE NOR GRAND, BUT WAS ROOMY ENOUGH TO HOLD THE FEW TREASURES THAT MY PARENTS AND IMMIGRANT GRANDPARENTS HAD ACCUMULATED. IN A PLACE OF HONOR SAT OUR ONLY REAL HEIRLOOMS—MY GRANDPARENTS' RUSSIAN SILVER KIDDUSH CUPS, WHICH I STILL CHERISH TODAY. SETTING THE TABLE WAS NEVER A CHORE FOR ME BECAUSE I RELISHED TAKING THE "GOOD THINGS" OUT OF THE CABINETS AND DRAWERS OF THE BREAKFRONT AND SIDEBOARD, PART OF OUR NEW DINING-ROOM SET. GATHERING THE CUTLERY FROM THE SILVER-SERVICE BOX, SELECTING THE TABLECLOTH, FOLDING THE NAPKINS, ARRANGING THE GLASSES, BEING CAREFUL NOT TO BANG THE DISHES, EVEN PULLING OUT THE HEAVY TABLE PADS AND ADDING LEAVES TO THE TABLE WERE TASKS THAT BROUGHT ME PLEASURE AND SATISFACTION. I LOVED THE SHEER BEAUTY OF THE ROOM WHEN I WAS DONE, THE QUIET, EXPECTANT HUSH, THE AN-

TICIPATORY FEELING OF THE EVENT ABOUT TO TAKE PLACE. THIS BOOK, I HOPE, CAPTURES THE ESSENCE OF THE SPECIAL AFFECTIONS AND MEM-ORIES I HAVE ABOUT THE DINING ROOM AS THE HEART OF FAMILY LIFE.

ALTHOUGH I LOVE ANTIQUES, I AM NOT BY NATURE A COLLECTOR. I TEND TO BUY WHAT I NEED AND WHAT I KNOW I WILL USE. I'VE ALWAYS THOUGHT THAT BUYING THINGS JUST TO SHUT THEM UP IN A CABINET AND NEVER ENJOY THEM WAS AN AWFUL SHAME. RESERVING THE BEST FOR COMPANY DOESN'T MAKE SENSE TO ME EITHER—THE GOOD THINGS WE HAVE GIVE PLEASURE TO OUR FAMILY AS MUCH AS TO OUR GUESTS. ANTIQUES ARE SIMPLY EVERYDAY OBJECTS THAT HAVE MELLOWED WITH AGE. THEY COULD BE CALLED THE ULTIMATE RECYCLING EFFORT.

I SUPPOSE MY CAREER AS A CONSULTANT AND JOURNALIST IN THE FASHION WORLD, WHERE CREATING OBSOLESCENCE IS TOO OFTEN THE GOAL, HAS MADE ME LONG FOR SOMETHING THAT ISN'T INSUBSTANTIAL OR PART OF A TREND. BUT THIS DESIRE TO APPRECIATE THE GOOD LIFE—AND I DON'T MEAN NEW CARS AND FANCY STEREOS—ISN'T JUST MINE. AS THE YEARS SPEED BY, EVERYONE SEEMS TO BE REACHING BACK, TRYING TO HOLD ONTO AS MANY MEMORIES AND MEMENTOS AS THEY CAN TO CUSHION THE TRANSITION INTO A NEW MILLENNIUM. SURROUNDING OUR ANSWERING MACHINES, FAXES, AND COMPUTER SYSTEMS, ANTIQUES CAN SOFTEN THE HARD EDGES AND ADD COMFORT AND QUALITY TO CONTEMPORARY LIVING, USUALLY AT A COST LESS THAN BUYING COMPARABLE ITEMS NEW. ANY CONTEMPORARY TABLE SETTING ACQUIRES ADDED DISTINCTION WHEN MELLOWED BY THE WONDERFUL PATINA

OF ANTIQUE SILVER, CRYSTAL, AND CHINA. ANTIQUES NEED NOT BE RARE OR OF MUSEUM QUALITY TO ENHANCE ONE'S LIFE. ONCE YOU BEGIN LOOKING, YOU'LL DISCOVER WONDERFUL OLD MATERIALS AND EXQUISITE WORKMANSHIP IN THE MOST ORDINARY TABLEWARE OF TIMES PAST. AND EACH OBJECT TELLS A STORY. EVEN THE SMALLEST DISHES AND CUPS REMIND ME OF THE PLACES I FOUND THEM—THIS FUNNY TEAPOT IN A POKY SHOP IN THE CITY, THAT BASIN ON AN OTHERWISE DISCOURAGING RAINY DAY, THIS PITCHER AT AN ESTATE SALE IN A NEARBY COUNTRY TOWN.

THE INHABITANTS OF THE REGION AROUND THE BERKSHIRE HILLS, IN THIS NORTHWESTERNMOST CORNER OF MASSACHUSETTS, ARE AS WARM AND WELCOMING AS THE COUNTRYSIDE. WHAT I LOVE ABOUT THIS AREA ARE THE WONDERFUL ROLLING HILLS, OPEN GREEN FIELDS DOTTED WITH COWS, AND BEAUTIFUL RAMBLING OLD FARMS AND POCKETS OF TIDY VILLAGES. SINCE MY HUSBAND AND I CAME HERE SEVENTEEN YEARS AGO, WE'VE ENJOYED THE CALM BEAUTY, THE WARM ATMOSPHERE, AND THE RICH TRADITION. UNLIKE MANY OTHER SUMMER COMMUNITIES, THE BERKSHIRES, EVEN IN THEIR MOST GILDED AGE, HAVE ALWAYS BEEN "THE COUNTRY." (CAROLE OWENS, AUTHOR OF THE EXCELLENT BOOK THE BERKSHIRE COTTAGES, COMPARED THE FABULOUS HOUSES BUILT BETWEEN 1880 AND 1920 TO "PENNIES FLASHING IN THE HIGH GRASS.") BUT THE NUMEROUS CULTURAL INSTITUTIONS FLOURISHING IN THIS REGION TAKE IT ABOVE AND

BEYOND THE PURELY BUCOLIC, GIVING IT A UNIQUE AND INTERNATIONALLY KNOWN REPUTATION: FOR MUSIC, THERE'S TANGLEWOOD, THE FAMOUS SUMMER HOME OF THE BOSTON SYMPHONY ORCHESTRA, WHICH DRAWS THOUSANDS OF VISITORS EVERY YEAR (UP THE ROAD IS WHERE ARLO GUTHRIE COMPOSED "ALICE'S RESTAURANT"), THE BERKSHIRE OPERA, AND THE ASTON-MAGNA FOUNDATION; FOR THEATER AND DANCE, THE WILLIAMSTOWN AND BERKSHIRE PLAYHOUSES, THE SHAKESPEARE FESTIVAL, AND JACOB'S PILLOW; FOR ART AND ANTIQUES, THE HANCOCK SHAKER VILLAGE, THE OLD MISSION HOUSE, THE STERLING AND FRANCIS CLARK MUSEUM, THE NORMAN ROCKWELL MUSEUM, AND NUMEROUS ANTIQUES FAIRS, AUCTIONS, AND ARTS-AND-CRAFTS SHOWS.

THE BERKSHIRES COMPRISE TWELVE TOWNS, OF WHICH STOCKBRIDGE AND LENOX ARE THE MOST FAMOUS. THE LITERARY WORLD DISCOVERED THE BERKSHIRES IN THE 1830S, WITH THE PUBLICATION OF CATHERINE SEDGWICK'S IMMENSELY POPULAR NEW ENGLAND TALES, AND CENTERED ITSELF AT STOCKBRIDGE. (THE SEDGWICKS HAVE REMAINED ONE OF THE PROMINENT FAMILIES IN THE AREA;

CATHERINE'S DESCENDANT EDIE MADE HISTORY OF HER OWN IN THE 1960S.) NATHANIEL HAWTHORNE LIVED IN THE LITTLE RED HOUSE ON STOCKBRIDGE BOWL, WHILE HERMAN MELVILLE LIVED AT ARROWHEAD IN PITTSFIELD, JUST DOWN THE ROAD FROM OLIVER WENDELL HOLMES. OTHER PERMANENT AND TEMPORARY RESIDENTS HAVE INCLUDED HENRY WADSWORTH LONGFELLOW, HENRY DAVID THOREAU, DANIEL WEBSTER, THEODORE ROOSEVELT, AARON BURR, AND MARK TWAIN. NEWS OF THE "LAKE DISTRICT OF AMERICA" BROUGHT OTHER CONTRIBUTORS TO THE WORLD OF ARTS AND LETTERS: MATTHEW ARNOLD, HENRY JAMES, OWEN WISTER, FREDERIC CROWNINSHIELD AND FRANK CROWNINSHIELD, THOMAS SHIELDS-CLARKE, SUSAN METCALFE, LYDIA FIELD EMMET, AND ROBERT EMMET SHERWOOD AND ROSINA EMMET SHERWOOD. IN STOCKBRIDGE, THE SCULPTOR DANIEL CHESTER FRENCH SPENT SIX MONTHS OF THE YEAR AT HIS COUNTRY ESTATE, CHESTERWOOD, AND AMBASSADOR JOSEPH HODGES

CHOATE HIRED MCKIM, MEAD & WHITE TO BUILD THE RAMBLING SHINGLE-STYLE HOUSE HE CALLED NAUMKEAG; IN LENOX, EDITH WHARTON ESTABLISHED HERSELF AT WHAT SHE CALLED "MY FIRST REAL HOME," THE MOUNT. ALL ARE OPEN TO THE PUBLIC TODAY.

THE REGION'S LITERARY AURA AND NATURAL BEAUTY DREW AN INCREASINGLY WELL-HEELED CROWD, UNTIL THE AREA CAME TO BE CALLED "THE INLAND NEWPORT." A STOP AT LENOX BECAME PART OF SOCIETY'S YEARLY SCHEDULE, IN WHICH JUNE AND JULY MEANT NEWPORT, AUGUST MEANT SARATOGA FOR THE WATERS AND HORSES, SEPTEMBER AND OCTOBER WERE SPENT IN THE BERKSHIRES FOR THE FALL FOLIAGE, AND THEN ONE WENT ON TO NEW YORK CITY IN NOVEMBER FOR THE THEATER. THE FOUR HUNDRED, AS THEY WERE CALLED, WERE THE ELITE—THE VANDERBILTS, THE ASTORS, MARSHALL FIELD, GEORGE WESTINGHOUSE, MARK HOPKINS, ANDREW CARNEGIE, J. P. MORGAN, HARRY PAYNE WHITNEY, AND THE LIKE. THEY WERE ALL MILLIONAIRES, AND MANY OF THEM BUILT EXTRAORDINARY MONUMENTS TO THEIR ERA. DURING THIS PERIOD, LAND PRICES ROSE FROM $50 TO $1,000 AN ACRE. THE NAMES OF THE HOUSES THEMSELVES ARE LIKE ECHOES FROM THE PAST: ELM COURT, WHOSE DINING ROOM SAT FIFTY; WHEATLEIGH, NOW A RENOWNED RESTAURANT, WHOSE OWNER, MRS. DEHEREDIA, WAS THOUGHT TO BE THE MOST GRACIOUS HOSTESS IN THE BERKSHIRES; BELLEFONTAINE; WYNDHURST; BROOKHURST; BLANTYRE, WHICH IS NOW ONE OF AMERICA'S FOREMOST COUNTRY INNS; ERSKINE PARK, WHERE EVERY DRIVEWAY WAS SUPPOSEDLY COVERED IN WHITE MARBLE CHIPS. OF THE NINETY-THREE "COTTAGES" SPRINKLED THROUGHOUT THE TWELVE

TOWNS, MANY WERE RAZED OR HAVE DETERIORATED FROM NEGLECT. SOME HAVE BECOME CHURCHES, SCHOOLS, HOTELS, AND

MUSEUMS. A VERY FEW REMAIN IN PRIVATE HANDS.

SEVERAL YEARS AGO, MY HUSBAND AND I HAD A CHANCE TO ACT ON A DREAM. WE ALWAYS DREADED HEADING BACK TO NEW YORK

CITY FROM OUR HOUSE IN THE BERKSHIRES ON SUNDAY EVENINGS, SO WE DECIDED TO COMBINE OUR LOVE OF ANTIQUES

AND THE BERKSHIRES AND OPEN A SHOP IN GREAT BARRINGTON, THE COUNTRY DINING ROOM, WHICH FEATURES NOTHING BUT

ANTIQUES FOR THE TABLE. WE MAY HAVE COME TO ANTIQUES DEALING BY AN UNCONVENTIONAL ROUTE, BUT WE ARE PROOF OF THE

JOYS OF LIVING WITH ANTIQUES. WE QUICKLY REALIZED THAT WITH SIX ADULT CHILDREN AND THEIR FRIENDS, EVERY MEAL AUTO-

MATICALLY BECOMES A DINNER PARTY, AND DINNER CONVERSATIONS BECOME MINI HISTORY LESSONS ON HOW AND WHY A MARROW

SPOON, FISH CARVER, SUGAR SHAKER, AND MANY OTHER ONCE POPULAR SERVICE PIECES WERE USED. THIS BOOK FOCUSES ON THE SUR- ROUNDINGS, AMBIENCE, AND TABLE ACCESSORIES THAT MAKE EATING AS SATISFYING A PLEASURE FOR THE EYES AS FINE FOOD AND WINE ARE FOR THE PALATE. WE PHOTOGRAPHED ANTIQUES RANGING FROM ABOUT 1770 TO 1920, MAKING A CONSCIOUS EFFORT TO SELECT OBJECTS THAT ARE READILY AVAILABLE AT GOOD PRICES. (TECHNICALLY, AN ANTIQUE IS AN OBJECT AT LEAST ONE HUNDRED YEARS OLD, SO SOME PIECES OF

WHAT WE'VE SHOWN ARE ACTUALLY THE ANTIQUES OF TOMORROW, WHICH CAN BE CONSIDERED EXTRA-GOOD BUYS TODAY.) MUCH

OF THE CHINA IN THESE PAGES IS ENGLISH, A RESULT BOTH OF PERSONAL TASTE AND OF THE STYLE SUGGESTED BY THE COUNTRY-

HOUSE FEEL OF THE BERKSHIRES. AS WE WEREN'T INTERESTED IN PERFECT PERIOD DETAIL, WE SOMETIMES LET OUR IMAGINATIONS RUN

WILD WHEN WE SET THE TABLE; WE RECOMMEND YOU DO THE SAME. THOUGH THE FOLLOWING PAGES OFFER A COMPREHENSIVE

OVERVIEW OF ANTIQUE TABLEWARES, OUR AIM IS AS MUCH TO INSPIRE AS TO EDUCATE. DISCOVERING AND REVIVING THE GRACE AND

LUXURY OF EARLIER ERAS IS A HEARTENING ENDEAVOR. OUR JOURNEY BACKWARD IS REALLY A JOURNEY AHEAD, AND OUR FUTURE GAINS

LIFE FROM ALL THAT WE HAVE LEARNED FROM THE PAST.

"ONE MAY LUNCH IMPERSONALLY WITH COMPARATIVE

STRANGERS; ONE MAY DINE FORMALLY TOUCHING

ELBOWS WITH ONE'S DEAREST FOES," AGNES MORTON

WROTE IN HER SLENDER 1894 *ETIQUETTE,* "BUT ONE

DOES NOT OF CHOICE BREAKFAST WITH ANYONE BUT

BREAKFAST

A FRIEND." BREAKFAST IS SPECIAL IN THAT IT IS GOV-

ERNED BY NO RULES EXCEPT THOSE OF PREFERENCE

AND EXPEDIENCE. FOR MANY OF US, BREAKFAST PRE-

SENTS OUR ONE CHANCE OF THE DAY TO BE ALONE,

AND WE CHERISH THESE PRECIOUS MINUTES, DRINK-

ING OUR SOLITARY CUP OF COFFEE ON THE PORCH

OR ENJOYING A FRAGRANT PIECE OF MELON ON AN

old blue-and-white porcelain saucer. Edith Wharton extolled the pleasures of a tray in bed—she knew that once she got up she would be besieged with demands on her time, and so she spent the morning writing in the safety of her room. For others, breakfast is a good-natured slapdash family event, with children, children's friends, and neighbors dropping in. Whether you have breakfast alone or in company, it's important to remember that the conveniences of modern living can blend very successfully with antiques: an individual coffee maker can be fitted over a fine old porcelain cup, old silver or wood trays can carry all the necessary boxes of cereal into the dining room, and orange juice tastes even better in a cut-glass goblet.

In Victoria's reign, breakfast saw its heyday. As industrialization brought affluence, people on both sides of the Atlantic sought ways of displaying their wealth, and food—and its accoutrements—became firmly established as a status item. By the mid-1800s, breakfast had become a full-fledged event, with meats, fish, game, dozens of egg dishes, pancakes, muffins, and toast all being served up on the side-board. Condiments spun happily on lazy Susans, and etiquette-book writers instructed housewives to "make a pretty glass dish, or silver or wicker basket of peaches, pears or plums, an institution of the summer breakfast."

Though the cookbook writer Marion Harland suggested in 1875 that "the American breakfast should be a pleasing medium between the heavy cold beef and game pie of the English and the too light morning refreshment of the French," many Americans followed the British lead, in manner if not in menu. This was especially true in the great houses, the enormous "cottages" of Newport, Bar Harbor, the Hudson Valley, and the Berkshires. "Breakfast, at which our grandmother was always present in a lovely negligee, was set in English fashion on a marble-topped sideboard," remembered a grand-daughter of Emily Thorn Vanderbilt Sloane White, mistress of the ninety-four-room Elm Court in Lenox, Massachusetts. Through both her marriages, first to the manufacturer William Sloane and then to Ambassador Henry White, Emily Thorn Vanderbilt was known as a gracious but punctilious hostess. She kept precise hours and demanded that her guests do the the same (she was famous for running her household according to a tight schedule posted in the hall). We can imagine this venerable matron holding court over the breakfast china, the cuffs of her lacy robe drooping dangerously near the jam.

At some of the great houses, such as Highlawn, which belonged to Emily Thorn Vanderbilt's daughter, and Elm Court, where visitors had name tags on their doors, guests were expected to show up promptly for breakfast and then sign up for a day of strenuous activities, from riding in one of twenty-eight vehicles to croquet, tennis, billiards, bridge, or ice skating and curling in winter. At Naumkeag, Ambassador Joseph Hodges Choate's shingle-style house in Stockbridge, the attitude was a little more lenient. Guests rang downstairs to the pantry for breakfast, and were sent up a tray loaded with one of the household's numerous china services. Though this treatment is a bit lavish for most of us, we can adapt it to today's needs. One idea is to assign guests their own special teacups and saucers, preferably unmatched pieces;

it's a nice way to use odd bits of pretty china, and gives a guest, especially a frequent visitor, the homey, comfortable feeling of having his or her own set. Another option is to prepare breakfast trays the night before, with cup, saucer, glass, bowl, napkin, and even a tiny bouquet of flowers if you like, and leave it on the kitchen counter or dining-room table; set out tea bags, kettle, and coffeepot and let your guests know where milk, cereal, and juice are so that they can help themselves and enjoy breakfast in the privacy of their rooms. This is an excellent way to make people feel welcome without

intruding on their morning privacy, especially if your guests are early risers and you prefer to sleep late yourself.

Whether presented on a tray or in the dining room, breakfast in the nineteenth century was served on informal china, since finer porcelains were reserved for dinner and entertaining. Today, these simple Stafford-shires—

Previous pages: Built in Lenox in 1903 by Mr. and Mrs. Robert Warden Paterson, Blantyre is now an exquisite hotel. In the conservatory, breakfast is set with an ornate Victorian silver teapot and a grand, quite early (perhaps late 1700s) hand-painted china pattern that picks up the gleam of the flatware. The size of the sugar bowl, much bigger than most made today, attests to the sweet tooth of previous generations.

A simple late-1800s two-color ironstone pattern like Genoa, produced by J. & G. Meakin in England, an ordinary fork, and a bakelite-handled knife serve for everyday breakfasts.

brown-and-white, blue-and-white, or red-and-white—or plain white ironstone add a note of freshness and familiarity to the morning. Odd plates in spatter-, sponge-, and mochaware jumbled about on the table look casual and sprightly, while earthenware (red, yellow, and white) goes well with big, hearty all-American breakfasts. Silver "hotel" ware or "train" ware from the 1930s—the actual coffeepots and teapots that serviced institutional tables and railroad dining cars across America—has a utilitarian yet stylish look, and blends well with earlier patterns. Special

Breakfast invites inventiveness. Soup bowls make good cereal bowls and a pressed-glass compote serves nicely for sugar. The flatware has a mixture of ivory and bakelite handles.

wooden pieces made for the table, referred to as treen (of a tree), are often extremely simple but beautifully crafted. These smooth wooden eggcups, trays, and other objects are very desirable and also mix well with china patterns and other table accessories.

The 1785 arrival in New York Harbor of the *Empress of China*, the first American ship to trade directly with China, started a century-long love affair with inexpensive blue-and-white Canton ware. Though there were enough different sizes of Canton ware to serve every meal, it was especially suitable for breakfast, with large cups and saucers, a sugar dish and stand, milk pot, teapot, slop bowl (for the tea dregs), and plates (seven to eight inches in diameter). A coffeepot, butter boat, and stand rounded out the service. In the late eighteenth century, the development of transfer printing made it possible for pottery firms to mass-produce items with fancy decoration. Some early transferware sets imitated China trade wares, with their blue landscape scenes, but by the 1820s pink, green, yellow, brown, black, or purple architectural, botanical, and commemorative designs were available as well. By 1850, breakfast dishes had become incorporated into larger sets of china, but a

Fresh fruit complements the lively colors of this ironstone pattern, made in the mid-nineteenth century by Brownfield & Son in England. Ironstone, a hard, white stoneware, is more durable than other types of china.

A sun room or a conservatory, like the one at this pleasant private home, is a delightful place for a leisurely family breakfast. An old drop-leaf table, eccentric, well-worn chairs, flowers plucked from the garden moments before, and nubby napkins all lend informality while an 1870s pressed-glass pitcher and gold-rimmed tumblers provide unexpected elegance.

well-off society matron at the dawn of the twentieth century might still have sipped her morning coffee or tea from her own individual silver service, elaborately festooned with her monogram. These special sets are fairly rare, but remember that any service made for tea or coffee (and there are many, in every possible variation) is appropriate for breakfast.

From the middle of the nineteenth century onward, enormous sets of everything—from suites of parlor furniture to butter knives—became the rage. If something existed on its own, the thinking went, it could only be better in quantity. Most china manufacturers responded to the prevailing love of completeness by producing breakfast dishes that corresponded to their popular patterns. These retained the shape and motif of the original dinner or tea service, only the plates were smaller and the cups were larger. With the table setting came a small cavalry of eating implements and serving dishes relating to breakfast foods. Services created exclusively for the deployment of breakfast are not easy to find these days. I once did see a Napoleonic three-piece boxed porce-

lain set, decorated with neoclassical scenes and eminently handy for taking along on campaigns.

As Mrs. Beeton attests, people ate eggs in every guise—scrambled, fried, poached, or baked. Small silver-plated tin or Britannia-ware canisters called egg coddlers or boilers allowed eggs to be cooked on the table; when done, the eggs were transferred to porcelain egg cups. Also popular were egg stands, which contained eggcups, matching gold-plated spoons (egg yolks corrode silver), and salt and pepper shakers. Since the 1770s, egg frames had kept eggcups warm in front of the fire before being brought to the breakfast table. The standard size held six eggcups, but special husband-and-wife sets of three existed: two eggs for him, one for her. Since egg frames in the early Victorian period quickly metamorphosed into grandiose, heavily ornamented objects that were extremely hard to clean, bone china became the egg-frame material of choice.

Occasionally, egg stands incorporated toast racks, but more often these stood on their own. They were made in every size and with every

Assorted blue-and-white and red-and-white Staffordshire dishes make a pretty pancake breakfast at Inn on the Green in New Marlborough, Massachusetts. Each plate is different, though all date from the 1800s. An 1830s blue willow leaf-shaped pickle dish contains sugar, a sugar bowl houses roses, and butter rests in another shallow Staffordshire bowl. The charming cow creamer—a form still popular today— dates from 1865. Other authentic touches include 1860 Tiffany & Co. silver pancake servers, a common wedding present in the Victorian era, and a pressed-glass syrup pourer. Unusual painted glass tumblers hold milk.

Unexpected accessories can enliven any table. Here, at Inn on the Green, an 1870 silver plate and oak wheelbarrow cruet—containing a cut-glass sugar caster, pepper shaker, and salt well, complete with shovel-shaped spoons—is ready to roll with a marvelous frosted lion's-head marmalade jar made in 1876 by the Gillander Glass Co. Though made a century later, a silver plate hotel-ware coffee service from the 1930s and new white cups and saucers are a perfect foil for the brown-and-white Staffordshire plates—and note the Staffordshire soup tureen holding the flower arrangement.

form of decoration, from the Gothic—all spiked arches and diamond cutouts—to the simple, classical lines of the early twentieth century. Mrs. Beeton recommends that dry toast (made from a loaf at least two days old) be placed in a rack and sent quickly to the table. Hot buttered toast, on the other hand, should be cut into triangles and arranged in piles on a warm dish. Most of us today are of the hot-buttered persuasion and may find toast racks, though delightful to look at, more useful for storing napkins or even letters.

When it comes to napkins, instead of trying to keep track of a full set, I like to use a mixture of patterns. I give each guest or family member his or her own napkin and assign a special silver napkin ring to keep it in. Traditionally, napkin rings were used to identify napkins that might be used for several meals before being washed—few housewives had enough time or supplies to present clean ones at every meal. A table set without napkin rings, on the other hand, implied that the linens were clean and would be washed before their next appearance at the table. We find, however, that reusing napkins from dinner at breakfast is perfectly acceptable and sensible. In our environmentally conscious era, we can't afford to waste any extra paper or wash water. Besides, napkin rings, however often you wash your linens, can be used to decorate the table—they were made in every style, and those with children or animals on top are especially fun to collect.

In the early nineteenth century, butter was stored in round ceramic tubs that kept it cool and protected. For serving it, people used silver items such as dishes, stands, or boats chased (decorated with fine lines) or engraved with flowers, shells, or Gothic motifs. Covered butter dishes in earthenware and pressed glass were ornamented with appropriate dairy motifs—a seated cow was a favorite. These Staffordshire and pressed-glass examples are now much in demand. Butter swirls, rolls, and pats, stamped with flowers, fern leaves, or shell designs, were both decorative and economical, and merited their own small dishes and knives. Butter was expensive, and providing each guest with one delicate creamy curl ensconced on a small silver or ceramic "butter-pat" ensured that no one would overindulge. Though butter is cheaper now, people tend to eat less of it, and these little pats are as useful today as they were then.

The development of packaged ready-to-eat breakfast cereal in the 1870s, pioneered by Dr. John E. Kellogg for his patients at the Western Health Reform Institute, and the entrepreneurial efforts of his brother Will, changed the face of American breakfasts forever. The genuine desire to reform eating habits, combined with the growing pressures of the business day, made the ease of ready-made foods especially appealing. Strenuous marketing efforts on Kellogg's part helped breakfast slip away from the grand meal it once had been. Today, of course, cereal is as much part of breakfast as coffee; elegant soup bowls from a dinner service that has been whittled away over the years are a wonderful, innovative way to serve cereal, and at the same time to enjoy antiques that might otherwise be relegated to a back shelf.

Today, few people have the time or inclination to hold formal breakfasts (unless we count the power breakfast, which we won't, or the weekend brunch, which we will), but the Victorians' love of ceremony and comfort can be a lesson for us. How we drink that first cup of coffee (out of a Styrofoam cup on the train or favorite porcelain at home) is very important. "Psy-

A delicious breakfast in bed at Aardenburg, an antiques-filled inn in Lee, features an English turn-of-the-century coffee set made by A. J. Wilkinson and earlier Wedgwood creamware egg cups on a lovely old oak and brass gallery tray.

chologically, the breakfast is peculiar," wrote Agnes Morton. "It is the first commingling of the day; and whether it be the late holiday feast, or the usual family gathering, it sets the pace for the twenty-four hours." We would do well to remember this. As for weekend entertaining, I love to bring out all our favorite items, mixed and matched on the dining-room table. Use a bacon fork for bacon, a fried-egg server for eggs, grapefruit spoons for grapefruit, and a pancake server—a popular novelty wedding present of the 1880s—for hot griddle cakes. Display fruit on a cake plate; put jam in a sparkling cut- or pressed-glass compote, sugar in a pickle dish, and flowers in a sugar bowl. Pour water from a silver pitcher, coffee from a porcelain pot, and milk from a tiny earthenware

jug. Mix contemporary white cups and saucers with brown-and-white Staffordshire for a gathering of the clan; for a romantic alfresco breakfast, use the most delicate Sèvres service, with tiny rosebuds popped in extra eggcups. Bring elegance to the setting but keep the atmosphere casual. Breakfast, more than any other meal, should be lighthearted. "No more hospitality can be offered than a dainty breakfast, especially in the country," Agnes Morton wrote, but cautioned, "Let not the hour be too early, for tired people are heavy sleepers; yet not too late, lest the heat of the sun may have become too suggestive of the approaching noon-tide; late enough for weary eyelids to unclose willingly, early enough for the fresh dewy odor still to cling to the vines on the porch."

LUNCH MAY BE, FOR MANY, THE HIGH POINT OF A

DULL DAY, BUT IT DOES NOT EVOKE THE PASSION OF

A MEAL LIKE BREAKFAST, SAY, OR TEA. PERHAPS THIS IS

BECAUSE WE ASSOCIATE IT WITH THE LUNCH BREAK,

THE HURRIED RUSH OF THE OFFICE DAY, THE INDI-

GESTIBLE BUSINESS LUNCH. YET LUNCH CAN BE ONE

OF THE MOST GRACEFUL TIMES TO ENTERTAIN:

A DELICIOUS SUMMER SALAD PLUCKED FROM

LUNCH

THE GARDEN AND SERVED ON HAND-PAINTED BOTAN-

ICAL PLATES; AN OMELETTE SERVED ON SPATTER-

WARE; BREAD, CHEESE, AND GRAPES ON COLORFUL

CHINA IN A TERRACE GARDEN; ASPARAGUS SPEARS

SERVED ON FRENCH DISHES DESIGNED ESPECIALLY

TO HOLD THEM. THE BEAUTY OF LUNCH IS THAT

ONE NEEDN'T BE A GOOD COOK TO SERVE A CHARM-

ING MEAL—WE NEED ONLY A LITTLE IMAGINATION

AND CREATIVITY. OF ALL MEALS, LUNCH HAS THE

FEWEST TRADITIONS AND SHORTEST HISTORY.

This page and previous pages: Sculptor Daniel Chester French spent summers at Chesterwood with his family for thirty-three years. Lunch in a trellised nook of his terrace includes a hand-painted 1840s Minton tureen and dishes delicately veined and shaped like curling leaves. Intended for serving dessert, the service seems most appropriate for a light luncheon of salads. The flat centerpiece of hosta leaves slides gracefully into the painted circle on the table, which echoes the garland swags painted on the wall by French's sister-in-law, Alice Helm French. Evoking elements of the sea, the flatware mixes mother-of-pearl handles with shell-shaped silver. A bust of the sculptor's daughter, who, in 1969, left provisions for the house to be turned into a museum after her death, overlooks the scene.

It sprang from humble beginnings; the word itself derives from "lump," the hunk of bread or cheese a worker might eat as a noontime snack. For centuries, a family's most important meal took place in the middle of the day and was called dinner; supper, from the French *souper* (a meal based on a delicious, hearty soup, or *potage*), was eaten in the late afternoon, followed by bedtime in the early evening. There is a thirteenth-century French saying that pinpoints the main meal of the day to nine in the morning: *Lever à cinq, diner à neuf, souper à cinq, coucher à neuf.* But in the last century, lunch, called "an unceremonious dinner" by one Victorian gentleman and "a lounging half meal" by another, began to take the place of the hot, heavy dinner. Etiquette-book writers, the guardians of manners, pounced on the idea, recognizing an opportunity to blend practicality, fashion, and moral rectitude. "The midday meal has always worn for me a grim and certainly unpoetical aspect," confessed Marion Harland, a prolific writer of household management books. "The 'nooning' should, for the worker with muscles, nerves, or brains, be a light repast and easily digested."

Far left and right: In an alcove off the dining room at Blantyre, green service plates from Limoges alternate with Royal Bavarian maroon plates. The floral dishes are Meissen and the small American celery dishes are from Lenox. Capo di Monte porcelain figurines (1800–1820) prance behind etched water goblets, green Steuben glasses, and gold-rimmed cordial glasses. At Blantyre, antiques are used at every meal.

Fruits and vegetables piled on a cake stand bring verve to this classic setting overlooking the Berkshire hills. Bouquets in cordial glasses echo the flowers painted on the gilded goblets, while the embroidered edges of the place mats fit perfectly on a round table. The mixture of English and French china includes, from top to bottom, Cauldon, England; Limoges, France; and Rouen, France.

Flatware specifically made for eating fish appeared in the early nineteenth century. Often ornately decorated, fish services generally have handles of bone, mother-of-pearl, or ivory, and engraving on the wide, flat blades of the knives (designed for separating bones from flaky flesh). This set dates from the late nineteenth century and has handles of carved ivory.

"I never in my early life came in contact with the gold-fever in any form," Edith Wharton wrote, "and when I hear that nowadays business life in New York is so strenuous that men and women never meet socially before the dinner hour, I remember the delightful weekday luncheons of my early married years, where the men were as numerous as the women, and where one of the first rules of conversation was the one early instilled in me by my mother: 'Never talk about money, and think about it as little as possible.'" Born into an old and prominent New York family, the Joneses (of "keeping up with the Joneses" fame), Edith Wharton spent some of her happiest years at The Mount, her house in the Berkshires. There she entertained Henry James, Walter Berry, George Cabot Lodge, and other lights of the literary scene. We can imagine these leisurely lunches, set with sparkling silver and elegant gold-and-white china, green-and-cream Coalport, or floral Haviland—lunches where the conversation and the setting were far more memorable than the food actually served. But by the second half of the nineteenth century, "gold fever" had struck most men in the rising middle and upper-middle classes; the industrial revolution and all its opportunities for building fortunes meant that men no longer had the leisure for lengthy midday dining at home. They left the house after breakfast and didn't return until evening, lunching at clubs or restaurants.

For women, the new technological changes meant increased freedom from household responsibilities. Lunches and teas became, as they are today, a chance for women to meet and discuss their common concerns. Though women eating alone or with their children would have a simple meal, a woman entertaining her friends might bestow on her luncheon all the elegance of a mini dinner party. "The formal luncheons for which engraved invitations are issued are usually 'ladies' luncheons,'" wrote Agnes Morton. "The formality of the serving is equalled by the elegance of the toilets." These parties, often with handwritten menu cards at each seat,

offered an appealing and substantial meal: bouillon (hot or jellied), little vols-au-vent of oysters, chicken, thin cuts of beef or cold sliced ham; salad; cheeses; and an array of small side dishes of condiments, relishes, and crudités. Prettily decorated cakes and molded ices finished the meal on a festive note. Today's ladies' luncheons differ more in the menu and conversation than in the setting and decor. In fact, contemporary society matrons are talking openly about money and how to raise more for their various charities. But it's easy to imagine the same floral Haviland that graced tables a hundred years ago at home in today's place settings.

Few items of tableware were invented specifically for lunch. Though luncheon sets did exist, they were often derivations of a matching dinner set, with smaller plates and forks. Even the linen napkins used for lunch were diminutive versions of their dinner cousins—fifteen inches as opposed to twenty-four. But a scarcity of matched luncheon sets gives all the more latitude for creativity at the table today. Even if you have a complete matched set of china, mixing china patterns provides an enormous range of ways to add subtle or dramatic touches to a meal. The most obvious way is to combine two patterns, one on the top plate, one on the underplate. In addition, alternating the colors of the underplates gives distinction to the table without being jarring. (For a more dramatic effect, use fully colored plates; for a subtle look, pick plates with simple colored bands around the rim.) Or alternate the colors of the top dishes. Antique dishes are especially effective when used as underplates for ordinary white china, thus reducing wear and tear on the older plates. Napkins and place mats also provide colorful accents, while a largish plain plate underneath something dainty adds punctuation and can act as a place mat.

A ladies' lunch in the music room, recreated here in a suitable setting at Aardenburg Inn, might find Duncan Phyfe lyre-back chairs harmonizing with the piano-forte and bronze dolphin candlesticks setting the tone for the fish course. Green cased glass salt cellars and wine glasses pick up the subtle palette of the 1880s Doulton soup and luncheon service. In the corner, an 1840s French bronze and glass tiered cake stand offers goodies for dessert.

On this 1750 walnut
Queen Anne drop-leaf
table are bold blue-and-
white plates crafted by
Dedham art potters in
the early 1900s, nine-
teenth-century floral
dessert dishes hand-
painted in Leeds, Eng-
land, and simple
American spongeware
plates. A bountiful
arrangement fills an old
redware platter, and an
early European silver
pepper grinder waits on
ivory feet across from a
pewter mustard pot.
Batik napkins contrast
with the collage of ori-
ental rugs at this lovely
private home.

What the high-style luncheon lacked in heaviness, it made up for in expansiveness, with dozens of choice morsels to tempt skittish appetites. All the condiments and crudités required their own serving utensils and plates—celery vases for celery (which became floral arrangements in their own

Right: The sparkle and freshness of pressed glass adds coolness to a summer buffet. Filled celery vases become an alternative flower arrangement.
Far right and following pages: The full repertoire of accessories displayed at this lovely Berkshires home consists of hand-painted asparagus plates from Limoges, France; individual English asparagus tongs; and a pair of larger asparagus servers (see following pages) made by Gorham. Green depression glass plates, cut-glass goblets, finger bowls, and American flatware complete the picture.

right), strangely pronged silver forks for tomatoes (steel was thought too acidic), scoops for Saratoga (potato) chips and oyster crackers, and an endless array of clear and colored pressed- or patterned-glass dishes. The Victorian was an era when people pickled everything—peaches, pears, apples, cherries, plums, cucumbers, beets, cauliflower, cabbage, nasturtiums, walnuts, onions, mangoes, eggs, and tomatoes—and each colorful condiment needed its own saucer, compote, or bowl. "Lunch without pickles of some kind is incomplete," remarked *Good Housekeeping* in 1889. Today we don't serve as many condiments, but the pressed-glass dishes are useful for everything from ketchup to nuts to potpourri. A profusion of them catching the light brightens any setting. I often use a glass cake stand as a centerpiece; it's fun arranging fresh vegetables into an eccentric ensemble.

Our mania for bottled water may seem contemporary, but actually it echoes a similar fad a hundred years ago. Nineteenth-century Americans, many of whom abstained from alcohol and associated it with evil, venerated mineral water (tap water wasn't altogether clean yet) and served it regularly at lunch and dinner in silver or glass pitchers or carafes. Glass was especially popular because cut- or pressed-glass goblets were pretty and decorative for either wine or water.

In the country, it's sometimes difficult to regulate people's comings and goings, and lunch on the run is often a practical choice. Enormous blue-and-white Staffordshire platters loaded with sandwiches; tall pressed-glass pitchers filled with lemonade, iced tea, or sangría; a stack of plates; and a selection of napkins and tumblers make a perfect help-yourself atmosphere for people just in from a game of tennis or on their way out to go swimming. And in summer weather, there is nothing more delightful than eating outdoors in a shady spot, a vine-covered loggia, or a bright screened-in porch. Eating outside invites creativity and spontaneity and provides an opportunity to make the most of seasonal foods, the specialized items for serving and eating them, and the long, hot days when the sunlight dapples the maple leaves.

IN THE NINETEENTH CENTURY, EVERYONE KNEW THAT

DINNER WAS THE MAIN EVENT, AND HAD TO BE

ORCHESTRATED DOWN TO THE LAST DETAIL. "DINE

WE MUST," ISABELLA BEETON OBSERVED, "AND WE MAY

AS WELL DINE ELEGANTLY AS WHOLESOMELY." THE

MOST IMPORTANT OF SOCIAL OCCASIONS, DINNER

WAS THE VERY EMBODIMENT OF ALL THE VICTORIAN

ATTITUDES ABOUT EATING AND ENTERTAINING.

HOW—AND WITH WHAT—ONE DINED WAS A MEA-

SURE OF ONE'S STATUS. EVEN TODAY, DINNER IS

APPROACHED WITH SOME TREPIDATION. UNLIKE THE

HASTE OF BREAKFAST OR THE FRESH SIMPLICITY OF

LUNCH, DINNER REQUIRES MORE THOUGHT; IT'S

D I N N E R

harder to just pull something together. Still, to reassure the fainthearted, any meal looks, and tastes, better for being lovingly presented in beautiful dishes, whether the most elaborate service for twelve or three unmatched sets pulled together with colors and flowers.

Few people today could tolerate the sheer bulk of a Victorian dinner, let alone spare the hours it took to eat it. Still, we can appreciate and emulate the sentiments that gave rise to this gracious event—a love of hospitality, a celebratory feeling of family and friends coming together at day's end. After all, as Oscar Wilde quipped, "After a good dinner, one can forgive anybody, even one's own relations." The nineteenth century was the golden age of tableware, if not always in terms of quality, at least in terms of quantity. The configuration of cutlery that we use today—salad, fish, and dinner forks on the left, and, on the right, corresponding knives and a soup spoon, with a dessert spoon and fork above the plate—is based on the pattern set in the nineteenth century. However, even our most elaborate dinner setting is far simpler than its late-nineteenth-century equivalent.

Quirky details such as
sunflowers in a gold
bowl, flamboyantly
folded napkins, and a
wreathed bust of George
Washington keep this
young bachelor's annual
banquet lively. In addi-
tion to the 1910 Havi-
land service for eighteen
(the plates have an
unusual crinkly edge
and tree-and-well design
traditionally associated
with platters), a fabu-
lous complete set of
early 1900s cobalt and
gold Val St. Lambert
cameo glasses graces
each place. Note the
alternating chair styles,
English Regency cande-
labra, and imperial
gleam of the Swedish
chandelier.

Yet, interestingly, Victorian excess was coupled with an almost puritanical fastidiousness, and despite the customary enormous menus, it was considered disgusting to make any reference to the physical aspect of eating. Etiquette books instructed readers that openly enjoying food was indelicate, and that touching food directly with one's fingers was obscene. Scads of objects manufactured in the new mechanical processes—pressed glass, transfer-printed earthenware, silver-plated Britannia ware—presented diners with innovative and sophisticated ways to prevent food and fingers from touching, and whole subsets of objects came into being to accommodate the requirements of finicky diners. Some objects, such as knife rests in glass or silver, finger bowls and attendant doilies, and toothpick holders in every guise can be used today; others are usually considered oddities.

Enormous sets of silver and porcelain that formed place settings as we think of them today didn't exist until the first half of the nineteenth century, except those sets that were specially made for members of the court and aristocracy. Then, from about 1850 onward, manufacturers standardized not only sizes, as they had from the early 1800s, but also components of dinner sets, providing dinner, soup, breakfast, and tea plates (usually a dozen and a half of each per order), soup tureens, sauce boats, covered oval vegetable bowls or entree dishes, platters in varying sizes, dishes grooved with a tree-and-well design for capturing gravy, a round pudding dish, two deep oval dishes, a butter plate, custard cups, oyster plates, a salad bowl, and a pair of spittoons. Nowadays, of course, antique sets complete from dinner plates to butter plates to coffee cups are much less common than a stack of twelve plates, but such things have survived over the years better than one might think. Estate sales and country auctions are good places to look, and a complete set for twelve, unless it's a prize antique, is almost certain to be less expensive than buying the same pattern new—provided that it hasn't been discontinued.

We tend to think that a full service of china is required for the most formal

Here, at Aardenburg Inn, a mixture of patterns achieves an elegant formality. Flanked by giant five-armed candelabra, an epergne acts as centerpiece, with radiating side dishes holding strawberries. The bare mahogany table and wine rinsers at each plate (for a quick dip of the goblet between wines) evoke the Federal era.

dinner; in fact, depending on the floral arrangements, choice of glasses and silver, napkin colors, and so forth, a mixed set can appear as stately as a complete set. Napkins folded into ornamental shapes can dress up a table or add a note of whimsy, depending on how they're arranged. White-and-gold or cobalt-white-and-gold porcelain plates are as formal as it gets, and using a mixture of larger blue-banded plates and smaller gold-rimmed bread-and-butter plates with lace place mats or white damask linens will give a room all the dignity required. By the same token, a complete set can be made to seem casual. A bright purple in the place mats or a sophisticated apricot in the napkins, an unusual vegetable centerpiece, or a dozen sprigs of flowers in different types of glasses or even eggcups will make a room seem much more contemporary, no matter how loaded down it is with antiques.

Even the most ordinary or everyday set of china can be precious, and sometimes it's the items that were a dime a dozen way back when that we value today. The rage for the country look has gotten everyone to reconsider the old beat-up pieces of furniture out in the garage. The same thing has happened with ceramics: spongeware—the simple, and often quite crude, china of farmers' wives—is now admired for its texture, color, and character. Staffordshire and even blue-and-white export ware are other examples. Standard fare in the early nineteenth century, now they're highly desirable and rare; the more they were used, the less likely that any of them survived. Paradoxically, the finer, more delicate

porcelains are sometimes better preserved. In fact, they have lasted because they were valued, set aside for company dinners and stored in glassed-in cupboards. The precious china is around today because of its quality; the everyday china is around because of the prodigious quantities that were produced, and as a result there is something available for virtually every taste.

In one of his poems Oliver Wendell Holmes good-naturedly wrote that "the true essentials of a feast are only fun and feed." Both Holmeses, father and son, like other blue-blooded nineteenth-century gentlemen, appreciated the art of dining, which they practiced with such distinguished Berkshires neighbors as Nathaniel Hawthorne and Herman Melville. At Arrowhead, a cozy Federal house in Pittsfield, Melville supped with his family on his wife's yellow-and-blue Canton ware and wrote evocatively in *Moby Dick* (which was written in a room that looked out toward Mount Greylock) of "chowder for breakfast, and chowder for dinner, and chowder for supper." Warmed by his family circle, Melville lived a simple life, writing and looking after his livestock. He had moved by the time the first great houses were being built, and he wouldn't have recognized the "essentials" deemed necessary a scant few miles away, where dinner at home meant a footman behind each chair. Of all the grand dinner parties, invitations to Elm Court and Wheatleigh were perhaps the most desired. There was an unspoken if friendly rivalry between the two great hostesses, Emily Vanderbilt White of Elm Court and Georgie deHeredia of Wheatleigh, with guests often coming down in favor of the latter. When Mrs. White had finished eating, it's said, the course was cleared, while at Wheatleigh the dishes were passed until everyone had had his fill.

In inviting guests to intimate dinner parties, nineteenth-century hostesses were instructed to follow the ancient Roman rule—guests should not exceed the Muses in

In summers in the Berkshires, going to Tanglewood is a tradition, and preconcert suppers a ritual. In this house near the great summer-long music festival, classic Gorham Landsdowne flatware from 1917 mixes with 1813 maroon-edged plates by Wedgwood. The small saucers, based on an old design, are still being made today at Limoges. The glass sparkling on the table includes ewers, candlesticks, and particularly delicate 1920s depression glass goblets.

number or be fewer than the Graces. Although this was a popular saying, many hostesses invited larger numbers. Being late was not fashionable; in fact, guests generally arrived fifteen minutes *earlier* than the time written on their invitations. For a woman, there was a small corsage waiting; for a man, a boutonniere and a tiny gilt-edged card bearing the name of the woman he was to escort in to dinner. It was an era predating the invention of cocktails, and as soon as everyone was assembled, the host offered his arm to the most distinguished female guest and led the way into the dining room. The table was festooned with all manner of glass, candles, flowers, silver, and delicate porcelain. Resting on the elaborately folded napkin (which might contain a roll or bread) or propped up before each plate would be a stiff menu card, gilt edged and, depending on the formality of the occasion, either printed or written in calligraphy. A London journalist recommended placing a rose or violets alongside the menu card: "When conversation momentarily flags in any quarter, you will see the silent or stupid guest at once fly to his menu or rose, which are always there before him."

An interior designer's boldly graphic arrangement of patterns mixes dramatic 1820s English ironstone dishes by Mason with chinoiserie and Russian silver kiddush cups, used to hold snapdragons. Acting as place mats, some napkins are draped over the table's edge, while others are held by silver napkin rings. Cut and etched American glassware dates from the 1880s.

At Naumkeag, Ambassador Joseph Hodges Choate's shingled cottage, grand dinners might have included a set of 1825–1835 yellow-and-white Wedgwood tureens and a Coalport dinner service. Victorian candleshades on glass candlesticks protect the eyes, and comfortable mahogany and leather chairs ensure leisurely dining. The twentieth-century yellow claret glasses hail from Italy. Two stacked pressed-glass cake stands and a fruit compote make a wonderful tiered centerpiece.

A romantic dinner for two at Inn on the Green contrasts a sophisticated table setting—1899 Gorham silver candleshades, Tiffany's gracious flatware pattern Windham, a Marseilles tablecloth, 1920s pastel-colored plates by Minton, and a champagne bucket and stand set—with the rusticity of the colonial surroundings. The silver knife rests, little used today, protect the cloth between courses.

It is astonishing to see how soon he revives and joins again in the conversation. The pause is so much better occupied than by the ordinary process of munching bread" (advice hostesses might wish to heed today). By the early twentieth century, special menu and place-card holders, patterned after popular styles, had been devised in silver and porcelain. Today, these are fun to collect, particularly the exotic Art Nouveau holders that appear to be growing straight out of the table.

While manufacturers, responding to the aesthetics of the day, thought that the more embellished an object was—no matter how utilitarian or insignificant—the better, Victorian chefs, often imported from or trained in France, transformed ordinary foods into elaborate gustatory concoctions. With the menu in front of him, any guest perplexed by the food on his plate or the arsenal of cutlery to either side could identify and anticipate the eight or so courses that made up an average dinner party. Oysters came first, followed by two kinds of contrasting soup, clear and dark. Then fish, then roast(s), vegetables, "entrees" (meat dishes), and game, each with accompanying side dishes of

vegetables, sauces, condiments, and kickshaws (small savories, or appetizers, from the French *quelque chose*), then, finally, desserts. Thirty-five or forty separate dishes of various types of food were not uncommon at a dinner for eighteen or twenty people. One course alone might encompass a haunch of venison, pigeon pie, braised ham, boiled capons, a saddle of lamb, and a spring chicken.

In the first half of the nineteenth century, tables were loaded by course, with the main dishes at the head and foot, and the "side" dishes along each side; diners helped themselves and each other by passing items down the table. At the end of a course, servants carried away the used plates, serving dishes, and silverware, replenishing the table for the next round. Typically, two or three white cloths covered the table in layers, and when the top one became too messy, a layer was peeled off, giving rise to the expression "when the cloth was removed." If the table was in good shape, at dessert time the plates were set straight down on the bare wood. If the table was inferior or damaged, a thicker, colored cloth might remain. An alternative to this

messy, cluttered, and cumbersome method of table setting came in the form of *service à la russe* at mid-century, with servants offering platters from which each guest helped himself. This established the custom of serving from the left and clearing from the right. Hostesses never completely adopted this mode, but instead engineered the method we still use—preparing a fully loaded plate in the kitchen and setting it before each diner at the table.

In either case, fewer dishes littering the table left room for festive decoration in the form of floral centerpieces and ever-more-elaborate silver, glass, and porcelain "table furniture." As people were meant to talk only to those on their immediate left and right, it didn't matter how overwhelming a centerpiece was. Favorites were a luscious assortment of American Beauty roses, orchids mingled with lilies of the valley, or a froth of maidenhair ferns. (A truly elegant dinner would have smaller matching bouquets spread along the table.) Moss was frequently used in leafy and flowery constructions. A clear bowl of water lilies placed on a mirror lined with moss created the effect of an underwater par-

Nineteenth-century diners employed all manner of "table furniture" as decoration. This elaborate allegorical candelabrum and the many gold-rimmed glasses indicate from whence the Gilded Age received its name.

adise. Bonbons, olives, nuts, celery hearts, and other delicacies filled twisting epergnes, while tropical fruit in stemmed, shallow gilt-silver or cut-glass dishes called tazzas dotted the table. Dresden or Sèvres statuettes—of a child bearing a basket of fresh grapes, perhaps, or a shepherdess with ripe strawberries in her porcelain apron—promenaded down the table. Sometimes the table decorations got a little out of hand. At a dinner honoring President and Mrs. William McKinley in 1897 at Wyndhurst, Mr. and Mrs. Sloane's palatial residence in Lenox, the hosts created an intricate flag-and-eagle centerpiece out of flowers, which contained several fireworks timed to go off at a choice moment; unfortunately, the sudden explosion caused the president's wife to faint, and she had to be carried to her room.

"The two main objects of dessert," an 1860s fashion chronicler wrote, "are its fragrance and its effect by way of ornament." Dessert has traditionally been the grand finale to any meal, meant to please the eye as much as to sweeten the bloated stomach. In the eighteenth century, tradition called for enormous pyramids of fruit and pieces of china piled high on the dining-room table— contemporary accounts claim that in

Dessert services tend to be the most elaborate and decorative part of a dinner service and were traditionally banded in pastels and edged in gilt, with handpainted pictures of birds or fruit in the center. These French plates, marked E. V. Haugout & Co., each display a different fruit. Unusual porcelain compotes are also part of the service. Dainty silver fruit knives and forks have mother-of-pearl handles.

some houses door frames were enlarged to accommodate the towering creations. In addition to overwhelming the table, they were on occasion unsturdy; Madame de Sévigné, it's said, was holding one of her famous salons when the centerpiece toppled and the twenty or thirty pieces of china wedged into it came crashing down.

Dinner in the artist's studio at Chesterwood combines traditional objects—late-1800s bell-shaped cut-glass decanters, candle-shades, and four colors of glassware, pre-1850s green being the oldest—with innovative effects such as lacquered red onions on a bed of green moss. A variety of textures—linens embroidered in gold, a white runner, slipcovered William IV chair seats, twig place mats, heavy gilt Minton dishes, and prewar Royal Worcester soup bowls—keeps the atmosphere elegant and decidedly artistic.

Below: The 1850s Meissen pink-dragon dinner service has the same spiral quality as the nineteenth-century air-twist wine glasses. The hand-forged flatware is in the Kings pattern. This intimate family dinner in a private home is served on a drop-leaf table from Chippendale's workshop, accompanied by Queen Anne chairs dating from 1720.

Above: In the Chimney Room at Arrowhead, on the table where Herman Melville wrote Moby Dick, *a simple family supper has been set. Complementing this homey parlor are the circa-1860 Staffordshire earthenware pattern used by the Melvilles, napkin rings, 1850s glassware, simple flatware, and assorted ladderback chairs dating from the early 1700s to the mid-1800s. Melville's brother inscribed the author's short work* I and my Chimney *on the hearth.*

Following pages: Baby is included at this family dinner (highchair at left). Assorted brass candlesticks surround an 1870 mahogany lazy Susan holding a cruet set and condiments. Both the Tiffany flatware, called Broom Corn, and the complete set of Imari-patterned china date from the 1880s. The napkin folded to hold a dinner roll at each place was inspired by Mrs. Beeton's Book of Household Management.

Above: English majolica, a richly decorated earthenware inspired by earlier Italian pottery, became popular in the second half of the nineteenth century. This Minton pattern of pineapples incorporates unusual and marvelous serving pieces, shown to best advantage on a rustic table. The flatware is a mix of an 1895 pattern and 1920s ivorine-handled knives.

By the nineteenth century, pyramids had gone out of fashion, though flowers and fruit in every guise were still an important feature. It wasn't until the late Victorian period that a dinner service included dessert plates and coffee cups. Before that, dessert services were often the fanciest—and most fanciful—porcelain a family had. Sets included, in addition to at least twelve plates, a series of compotes in graduated heights, two or more cake plates, one or two sauce tureens with ladles and stands, and matching coffee and tea services, all in a pastel palette. Cut-glass and crystal vessels complemented the dessert service, and held brightly colored stewed and fresh fruit, sweetmeats, cakes, candies, and bonbons.

As Mrs. Farrar, an early American household adviser, notes from the heart: "A dinner, well performed by all the actors in it, is very fatiguing and, as it generally occupies three hours or more, most persons are glad to go away when it is fairly done." Even today, the real pleasure is to be able to think back on the glowing faces around your table and rest assured that your job *was* well done.

"UNDER CERTAIN CIRCUMSTANCES," HENRY JAMES

WROTE, "THERE ARE FEW HOURS IN LIFE MORE AGREE-

ABLE THAN THE HOUR DEDICATED TO THE CEREMONY

KNOWN AS AFTERNOON TEA." JAMES USED THIS

ADMIRABLE SENTIMENT TO OPEN HIS NOVEL *POR-

TRAIT OF A LADY*, PUBLISHED IN 1881, AND WE CAN

EASILY IMAGINE HIM SIPPING TEA OUT OF A DELICATE

THE ART OF POURING

TEACUP ON THE SHADED TERRACE OF THE MOUNT,

WHERE HE WAS OFTEN A GUEST. THESE DAYS, TEA IS

EXPERIENCING SOMETHING OF A REVIVAL; THOUGH

RARELY PART OF AN ORDINARY DAY (MOST PEOPLE

THINK THREE MEALS ARE PLENTY), ON A HOLIDAY,

WEEKEND, OR AS A SPECIAL TREAT, TEA PRESENTS

AN OCCASION FOR FESTIVE ENJOYMENT—ALL THE

MORE SPECIAL FOR BEING OUT OF THE ORDINARY.

Previous pages: Tea is set for two at Arrowhead on an 1840s cherry tilt-top table. Oliver Wendell Holmes, Herman Melville's neighbor, originally owned this 1870–1871 Gorham silver tea service, which includes an ivory-handled hot water urn and stand and is now part of the Arrowhead museum's collection. The cups and saucers are Staffordshire.

Left: Teapots come in every guise, from the homeliest brown earthenware to the finest, thinnest porcelain, and with all kinds of decoration. This magnificent 1890s tea service is mounted in an unusual silver frame.

Right: Tea strainers, which catch stray tea leaves before they flow into the cup, range from a traditional spoon shape to a bucket, the handles of which rest on the cup's edges, and the more new-fangled tilt-top style. Alternatively, silver tea balls—or eggs or miniature teapots— can be used to contain leaves as the tea steeps.

When tea first arrived from the Orient, it was expensive and precious enough to be stored under lock and key in wooden caddies, which were sometimes quite elaborate. (The term "caddy" derives from the Malay word kati, meaning a weight equal to 1–1½ pounds.) Here, from left: an 1840 oak tea caddy with two compartments for different types of tea; a marvelous 1770 George III fruitwood caddy fashioned into the shape of a pear; and a rare 1810 inlaid mahogany tea and coffee caddy, complete with a coffee grinder.

Above: The ritual of making tea calls for numerous accoutrements, many of which are small art objects in themselves. These caddy spoons, whose short handles allow them to be stored in the canister with the tea leaves, show a variety of high Victorian styles.

An heirloom silver tea service includes an elaborate tray, teapot, water urn, sugar bowl, and creamer, as well as a slop basin for the dregs and a coffee pot (both not shown). Collecting single teacups is a wonderful pastime, and a good way to accumulate an enchanting service that looks pretty in any combination. Though it's not necessary to know the makers to appreciate them, most manufacturers labeled their wares with the company's name, region, or, at the very least, the store that imported them. This collection contains pieces from the mid-nineteenth to mid-twentieth centuries.

Teacups and -pots with homey or patriotic sayings began appearing in England in Victoria's reign. This blue-and-white Camilla cup was actually designed for soup (hence its size) by Spode, which also produced the red cup at right and the blue one at left.

The late Ambassador Graham Parsons III collected all the cups on these pages as gifts for his aunt. The very small one at left is old Staffordshire and the white cup at center with a floral and gold motif is by Minton. Spode made the pink and gold cup; Aynsley produced the purple, the blue, and the yellow cups at bottom left.

A tea party is an opportunity to entertain a large number of guests (or just a few special friends) with ease. And now that people tend to eat dinner so late, a little something around 4:30 or 5:00 is welcome, reviving the spirit and feeding the stomach without spoiling the appetite for dinner.

When tea first made the long trek to England from China in the seventeenth century, it was hailed as a magical cure-all and was sold for exorbitant sums to the wealthy and cultured. Despite its prohibitive price (more than $100 per pound), the craze for tea swept all reaches of society, and by the eighteenth century, tea had become the national beverage (addiction, some complained). From the beginning, the tea ritual required its own paraphernalia. At first this consisted of a pot, small handleless cups (tea bowls) imported from the Orient or fashioned in Europe after exotic Eastern designs, matching deep saucers, a slop bowl for dregs, and a tea caddy in which to lock up the precious leaves. Made of wood, porcelain, or silver, caddies often came equipped with separate compartments for black and green teas

and a crystal bowl for mixing the blend. An elegant hostess would hold court over the caddy and, using a small silver scoop called a tea-caddy ladle, mix up individual blends for her guests. Those who found their tea too hot poured it into the deep saucer and drank straight from the dish. Mote spoons skimmed any unwanted leaves floating on the tea's surface; when they were turned around, their pronged handles freed up a congested spout.

Teahouses opened in England in the late eighteenth century, but it wasn't until 1840 that tea as a meal became an institution. Credit goes to Anna, seventh duchess of Bedford, who, suffering from a daily lassitude at about four, asked one afternoon for tea, bread and butter, and cake to be sent to her room. Afterward, she immediately perked up and made tea a daily ritual, inviting her friends to partake of her wonderful discovery. As with so much else, Victorian exuberance transformed this dainty refreshment into full-blown extravagance, with heaping platefuls of food and sideboards laden with dozens of cakes and biscuits. The queen herself

A hand-painted screen is the backdrop for tea in Edith Wharton's study at The Mount. The service, on a Pembroke mahogany tea table, is a beautiful 1830s Coalport. Silver tongs serve crustless sandwiches.

Chocolate pots, like this nineteenth-century English version, and coffeepots are similar in shape, both taller and thinner than teapots. But traditional chocolate is a thick drink, requiring a shorter, wider spout placed nearer the top of the pot than the longer, curved spout associated with coffee.

adored tea and made a comfortable ceremony of it at Buckingham Palace. Etiquette writers defined proper manners—spoon on the saucer, for example, if you want more, spoon in the cup if you've had enough. By the end of the century, in some great country houses tea was served in as many as five different rooms, with separate trays being sent to the drawing room for adults, the nursery and schoolroom for children and their governesses, the steward's hall for the "upper" servants, and the servants' hall for the "lower" members of the staff. In the years before World War I, teatime became even more refined, and was often held on grassy lawns with everyone milling around in beautiful whites, eating small crustless cucumber sandwiches and mounds of strawberries from silver platters.

In the United States, tea has somewhat different implications. As a drink, it has never excited the same passion as in England. As a meal, however, it was embraced by the rich and cultivated, many of whom were Anglophiles. Hotels began to serve afternoon tea, and gracious ladies gathered together to converse over dainty sandwiches and fine porcelain cups. Fashionable tea parties were a chance for women to unite, and for the sexes to mingle in a not-so-formal atmosphere and to flirt in acceptable circumstances. One was encouraged to talk to strangers, but not to stay more than forty-five minutes.

A properly laid tea table would have been a sparkling monument to excess even without the food. In addition to a caddy, sometimes in the form of a teapoy (basically a caddy set on tall wooden legs), a hostess would need a silver kettle and a corresponding tripod for boiling water at the table, or an urn if she was serving a crowd; a silver strainer; at least one teapot (most came in 1-quart and 1 1/2-pint sizes); a porcelain or bone china tea service and attending silver spoons; a tea

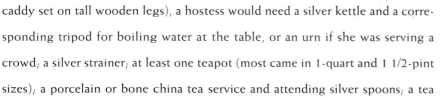

The easiest way to have coffee ready for serving immediately after dinner is to set up a sideboard. At Aardenburg Inn, these nineteenth-century demitasse and coffee services were made in England for Tiffany's.

Though sculptor Daniel Chester French's afternoon break consisted of crackers and milk, lemonade outside his studio at Chesterwood seems much more appealing. With the increasing availability of lemons and oranges throughout America in the nineteenth century, appropriately embellished citrus presses became popular. Once made, lemonade was served in ceramic jugs specifically decorated for that purpose or, more commonly, glass pitchers, like this 1870 American Bellaire design. The pressed-glass goblets have a stippled ivy pattern.

cozy if the setting wasn't too formal; a sugar bowl and tongs; a cream jug; cake stands and baskets; jam compotes; butter dishes; and sandwich platters.

The popularity of tea and the development of chinaware go hand in hand, each creating a demand for the other. The range of decorations and shapes in both china and silver tea services is as wide as the field itself. Like clothes and furniture, teapots have followed the styles of the era: oval-bodied or pear-shaped in the early eighteenth century, and often fashioned in the form of hens, tulips, or artichokes; classical in the late eighteenth century, such as those made from Wedgwood's jasper-ware—white figures standing in relief against an unglazed colored background, including the famous Wedgwood blue; and baroque, rococo, and neo-Gothic in the nine-teenth century. Tea gave license to flights of fancy, and teapots came disguised as everything from parrots to cauliflowers to cathedrals. Teacups and saucers matched the pots, and varied in shape and size as fashion decreed, with greater and lesser

degrees of success: at various points during the nineteenth century, teacups were made so wide-mouthed that they cooled tea poured into them almost instantly.

Henry Fielding's famous assertion that "Love and scandal are the best sweeteners of tea" didn't deter production of a whole host of apparatus to deal with sugar. For much of the nineteenth century, white sugar came in loaves or pyramids that had to be cut into small pieces with a cleaver and sugar nips. The lumps went into a large patterned silver or porcelain bowl on the tea tray and were transferred to the teacups with sugar tongs. If the sugar was ground fine in the kitchen, it might be put in a silver caster and scattered over a piece of cake. Today these silver casters, sugar sifters (pierced ladles), and sugar baskets make wonderful collectibles, imparting the elegance and tradition of days gone by to the tea table.

How to drink tea was much debated. Americans often drank it *à la russe* (poured directly onto a round of lemon) or iced with mint sprigs in tall glasses, while their English counterparts almost exclusively drank it with

Left: Cordial glasses, smaller versions of wine glasses that often have thicker stems, were introduced in the seventeenth century for drinking potent liquors. This elaborate eighteenth-century liqueur set, housed in its own wooden box and decorated with gold-leaf ivy designs, often traveled with its owner.

Right: A mahogany side table at Naumkeag has been set up as a bar, with a decanter set, here used for spirits, resting on a handsome Sheffield gallery tray. A bell-shaped nineteenth-century decanter and some twentieth-century sherry glasses are at left. A former biscuit box works as an ice pail with a pair of elegant clawed tongs. An embellished silver-topped water pitcher can be used for decanting wines.

milk or cream, poured from a silver or porcelain jug. Other concoctions included iced tea with Champagne and something unpleasant called "tea milk punch," made with a raw egg, said to be good for sufferers of the "cold stomach." Virtually all tea sets, of whatever material, provided matching creamers and sugar bowls, though again these can be acquired as individual pieces and used as one's fancy dictates.

Though cucumber, watercress, and smoked salmon sandwiches and bread and butter were standard features at teatime and had their own plates and platters, cakes, biscuits, and muffins made up a central portion of the meal.

These weren't the creamy, chocolaty cakes we eat today, but dry, light cakes seasoned with spices or seeds. Their ingredients were basic (butter, eggs, sugar, and flour), but their variations were endless. In *Breakfast, Dinner and Tea* (1869), Julia Andrews lists recipes for thirty-four cakes, from golden (with egg yolks) to silver (without) to pound, sponge, lemon, ginger, molasses, and Federal (raisin and brandy); Marion Harland, not to be outdone, offers fifty-two recipes. Served in silver cake baskets, on stands, or on glass plates, cakes could be eaten hot or cold, plain, or spread with butter and jam, which in turn

decorated the table in glass compote bowls or small white porcelain pots. While no one wants to duplicate a groaning Victorian tea table, a few choice sandwiches and a tasty Dundee cake, banana bread, or poppy-seed loaf, sliced and set on a silver cake platter, will make a delicious light repast.

A popular alternative to tea on hot summer afternoons was lemonade. As advances in technology and transportation made citrus fruit available across the United States, manufacturers produced numerous specialized implements, such as orange slicers and grapefruit spoons, to handle them. Squeezed by elaborately decorated citrus presses, lemonade was served in glass pitchers and appropriately ornamented frosted goblets or tumblers. Special accoutrements included long thin silver stirrers and sippers. For true lemonade, sugar cubes were rubbed with lemon rind and mixed with water, while an interesting drink called "white lemonade" consisted of lemon juice, sugar, white wine, and freshly boiled milk, all of which was strained through a flannel jelly bag, cooled, and set in ice. Specialized lemonade sets may be a bit hard to find today, but ordinary matching pitchers and glasses abound, and delightful groupings can be made with an assortment of different drinking vessels.

For winter afternoons, early Americans enjoyed cups of hot, thick, sweet chocolate, a beverage that has been somewhat neglected. Made from a thick paste to which milk was added, chocolate, cocoa, or cacao was a favorite drink for adults and children from the mid-seventeenth century onward. (Even Queen Victoria endorsed it, appearing in an advertisement for Cadbury's sipping a steaming cup of it as she relaxed in her well-appointed private railway car.) Frothy chocolate was made with whipped egg whites, while milled chocolate required churning the mixture in the pan with a whisk. A chocolate pot resembles a coffeepot in shape, in that it is taller than it is wide, but has a shorter, higher spout than a coffeepot, is a tad taller, and often has an aperture in the lid where milk can be poured in or a "muddler," "miller," or long swizzling spoon can be inserted to stir the mixture. A little of this concoction went a long way. Unlike today's hot chocolate, old-fashioned cocoa was a very thick drink, and three-quarters of a demitasse was plenty for most people. A very formal late-nineteenth-century tea set would include a teapot, a coffeepot, and a chocolate pot, but very special individual chocolate services can still be found. Some of the best came from Bavaria and Austria, places still known for their delicious chocolates and fine porcelains.

Chocolate and coffee arrived in Europe at about the same time—the mid-seventeenth century—and, following tea, vied with each other in popularity. The first coffeehouse in England opened in Oxford in 1650. Though initally coffee was most often consumed in public venues, it gradually became de rigueur at fashionable dinner parties. In 1861 Isabella Beeton remarked that consumption of coffee was growing daily, "especially since so much attention has been given to mechanical contrivances for roasting and grinding the berry and preparing the beverage." In the United States, coffee became far more popular than in England, with Americans consuming at mid-nineteenth century four times the amount of coffee as of tea.

Though most cookbooks of the day offered recipes for café au lait and for coffee with whipped cream, black coffee, thought to aid digestion, was the accepted after-dinner drink in social circles. "Fashion decrees café noir," wrote Agnes Morton, "and few lovers of cream care to rebel on so formal an occasion as a dinner; but when the formality is not too rigid, the little creamjug may be smuggled in for those who prefer café au lait." In her 1903 *Millionaire Households*, a half-admiring, half-critical peek at the lives of the "Smart Set," Mary E. Carter describes the java ritual: "The fair sex sit negligently about in the gilded salon sipping café noir from exquisitely decorated tiny porcelain cups into which they drop clear, amberlike flakes of rock-candy, cut sugar being too clumsy for this post-prandial beverage." Though tall coffeepots with long, serpentine, vertical spouts had been made for some time, coffee services came into their own in the 1880s, parallel to the growing popularity of "Turkish coffee," sets for which display a heady Arabic influence. Antique teapots are much more readily found than coffeepots, but a collection of the latter are especially handy now that most hosts like to offer both decaffeinated and regular coffee to their guests. Coffee cups came in two sizes: large breakfast cups (bigger than teacups) and demitasses, for after dinner. "Afternoon" coffee cups in the size we recognize today were also available and came as part of a matching tea set. "The mistress of the house," the great early-nineteenth-century food writer and epicure Brillat-Savarin declared, "should assure herself that the coffee is excellent, and the master, that the wines are of the best quality." Coffee originated in Ethiopia, but the word *coffee* actually derives from the old Arabic word *qahwah*, meaning wine; some food historians speculate that coffee was indeed the wine of the Muslims, whose religion forbids them alcohol. In any event, wine was as much a part of any evening dinner as coffee, requiring a different variety, in its own glass, for each course. At late- eighteenth-century dinners, guests had glass rinsers, into which they dipped their delicate vessels between courses, cleaning them for the next wine. These glass beakers can be extremely beautiful and, with small silver ladles, now make unusual sauceboats. By the 1880s, usually five glasses had come to adorn each place setting: a small one for sherry, to be served with the soup; a larger one for the Chablis, Hock, or Sauternes that went with the fish; a tall, thin one for the claret or Champagne that

A charming American silver-and-ivory corkscrew, its handle fashioned into a fearsome dog, dates from 1890. Corkscrews are marvelous items to collect, whether in active duty or not, and can be found with handles of silver, bone, wood, and ivory.

By cranking the handle on this uncommon 1840 English silver-plated bottle holder, wine can be decanted with little disturbance to the sediment. Like tea, wine has a wide range of paraphernalia associated with it. Note the cork with a silver chicken on top.

accompanied the roast; a fat, wide one for the Madeira or port that came after the game course, and a smaller sherry, claret, or Burgundy glass for the dessert wine. Sometimes one of the glasses was in an accent color, the most common being red or green. Any after-dinner Champagnes or sparkling wines were served just off the ice without decanting, a napkin wrapped around the wet bottle, or from tall, slender Champagne pitchers. Gilt-edged glasses were very popular for sparkling wines, and they are available today at modest prices; they add an extremely elegant touch to any dinner table.

Wine coasters, initially called wine sliders, came into being because raucous eighteenth-century diners, rather than calling in the servants, slid large bottles of wine across the table to one another, in the process nicking the table's smooth wooden surface. Coasters, most often made of wood and/or silver, also protected the table from wetness and rings. Their practical applications, however, were quickly overshadowed by the opportunities they provided for decoration—during the Victorian age, they became more

and more elaborately ornamented, until their original
function was all but forgotten.

Early wines and spirits came in thick, dark bottles
that obscured the contents; bottle tickets, small silver labels on chain-link cords, developed as a way to
identify the beverages. As decanting became more
and more pervasive and wine was served in cut-glass
bottles and decanters, wine labels turned into fancily
decorated items that paralleled the elegance of the
coasters. Other Victorian innovations were wine
casters and even wine wagons, which held several
glass decanters filled with wines or cordials; woven
silver wine baskets, which went about half or three-
quarters of the way up the bottle and were sometimes also used for seltzer; and
ice buckets and tubs. Traveling cases equipped with glass decanters and cordial
sets in wooden boxes were popular, bringing the amenities of home to far-off
places (or even to an overnight journey on the train). The other accoutrements
of wine—tastevins, ewers, pitchers, wine strainers, and corkscrews with handles
of silver, bone, wood, or ivory—were also embellished and fashioned in elaborate shapes and decorative designs.

Wine has never been as commonplace in the United States as in Europe (for
one thing, in nineteenth-century America it was four times as expensive as beer),
but as California emerges as a major wine center, interest has surged, particularly
in champagnes and sparkling wines. Newly engaged couples are given "wine
showers" by their friends to begin a wine cellar for their married life, while others have discovered wine tastings as a good focal point for a party. Whether your
interest is passing or passionate, graceful accessories for wine lend color and distinction to a room. New corkscrews may be easier to use, but an old bone-handled specimen has a status and dignity that no superefficient plastic model can
come close to.

*A sideboard at Aarden-
burg Inn is set with a
tall silver soda siphon,
a silver bottle stand, a
wine coaster, a round
cut-glass biscuit box for
ice, a tastevin, and an
ivory corkscrew with a
brush for flicking off
bits of old cork.
Following pages, left: A
cozy nook in the draw-
ing room at Blantyre is
the ideal spot for this
festive early-twentieth-
century Bavarian
chocolate set with cups
and saucers in four dif-
ferent colors.*

*Following pages, right:
The front parlor at Peir-
son Place, an inn in
Richmond, Mas-
sachusetts, still has its
original 1700s wallpa-
per. The eighteenth-cen-
tury mahogany tea table
has a "bird-cage"
design, meaning that the
top revolves as well as
flips up. The china
comes from New Hall, a
potters' cooperative that
started production in
the late 1700s in
Staffordshire.*

FOR SHEER ABUNDANCE, NOTHING RIVALS THE FULLY

LADEN BUFFET TABLE; IT SYMBOLIZES A SENSE OF WELL-

BEING, A FEELING OF PLENTY THAT ONLY THE MOST

CHURLISH COULD NOT RESPOND TO. BUFFETS ARE

OFTEN JOYOUS OCCASIONS CELEBRATING IMPORTANT

SPECIAL BUFFETS

MILESTONES: WEDDINGS, CHRISTENINGS, ANNI-

VERSARIES, CONFIRMATIONS OR BAR

MITZVAHS, GRADUATIONS. SOME-

TIMES THEY'RE TRADI-

TIONAL   HOLIDAY FEASTS OR

EVEN JUST A   HAPPY GATHER-

ING OF FRIENDS WHO   FIRST PREPARE

AN ENORMOUS MEAL AND   THEN REVEL

IN ENJOYING IT TOGETHER. OC-   CASION-

ALLY, OF COURSE, IT'S A FUNERAL

THAT BRINGS PEOPLE TOGETHER, BUT SAD

EVENTS TOO ARE PART OF LIFE'S MILESTONES.

BUFFETS ARE USEFUL FOR A NUMBER OF REASONS.

Previous pages and left: A grand occasion like a hunt breakfast, held in the front hall of a private home to herald the fall or celebrate the start of the hunting season, calls for lavish treatment, with details like silver pheasants poised to take flight and a richly colored old paisley shawl acting as a tablecloth. An 1815 ambassadorial Sheffield silver-plated soup tureen made by George Ashforth & Co. holds cider, meant to be poured with a Tiffany ladle into horn-and-silver beakers. A silver bone-handled pot brimming with nuts and, of course, a nut cracker continue the theme. A 1720 George I silver bowl contains shelled nuts, and a silver meat tray offers a savory delicacy. The Worcester plates are each handpainted with a different bird.

Above: Breaking bread in any season calls for boards and knives with decorative carving.
Right: For a sit-down meal, an exquisitely hand-embroidered cloth is set with tiny lead huntsmen and hounds and a turn-of-the-century Wedgwood hunt service handed down through the generations of one family. Special seasonal motifs can be incorporated, like the centerpiece of apples.

A festive, easy-to-pull-together lunch at another private home nearby cheers up a busy working day. Early 1800s Minton soup bowls serve as dishes for pasta salad, tossed in a big blue-and-white Staffordshire bowl. Silverware and extra napkins are available in a wooden tool box. Three 1860 Imari-patterned Mason ironstone pitchers in various sizes are stuffed with daisies. Kokomo patterned pressed-glass goblets and an array of covered cheese dishes on the back sideboard round out the picture.

A small buffet dinner for friends in a private home mixes and matches everything but the flatware, which is an unusual Chinese export silver. The plates all date from 1810 to 1840 and are English ironstone in various Oriental motifs. The goblets, all American pressed glass, date from 1850–1880. Chinese export napkin rings restrain bright damask napkins, emphasizing a color in each plate. Small enameled Battersea boxes provide each guest with a tiny flower arrangement.

Artfully combining mythology with abundance in the studio at Chesterwood, an English 1889 silver-plate presentation pitcher modeled as a bust of Juno explodes with flowers, and 1870s English majolica compotes fashioned as draped putti support fruit sculptures. Champagne cools in a Victorian jardiniere, and Stilton breathes in an 1860 English agateware cheese dish.

They require less outside help and, depending on the menu, can generally be prepared ahead of time, easing up on the pressures of last-minute arrangements. They are more spontaneous than sit-down dinners and are probably the best and easiest way to mix disparate groups of people. (They also eliminate the need for seating plans, though it's helpful if a host can provide some areas where guests can perch.) Guests can eat as much or as little as they want, and vegetarians can be accommodated without depriving meat eaters.

Called suppers in the nineteenth century, buffets were a popular midnight feature at balls, with cold meats, ices and other delicacies, and Champagne or punch to revive tired dancers. In the Berkshires, the young set danced till the wee hours at the Stockbridge Casino, now home of the Berkshire Theater Festival, and then returned home to tables loaded with enticing goodies. Today, buffets are still the most manageable way of serving large groups of people, and can be as elegant or casual as desired.

Most buffets are served in the dining room. The chairs are pushed

against the walls to provide better access to the table, which may be covered with a patterned cloth to disguise the inevitable spills and which holds food, plates, and cutlery. The cutlery can either be arranged in neat rows or wrapped in a napkin for each guest. A sideboard is indispensable, and might hold additional dishes of food, the drinks bar, or bread, salad, and other extras. Often the dessert is placed on the sideboard along with accompanying wines; after the main course, cakes and tarts can be moved to the larger table. Guests help themselves and usually eat in the living room, either at tables set up for that purpose or holding their plates on their laps. Whether you want to use your very best plates depends on how many guests you have. If the number of guests isn't too great, a buffet is an excellent opportunity to use stacks of eight or ten plates you adore; on the other hand, if the numbers are large, you might consider serving more pick-up and finger foods.

Sometimes the cause for a celebration is nothing other than the desire to observe the changing of the seasons. Or it can be a party based on a central theme—a beach party in January complete with imported sand, a Halloween dinner, or a hunt breakfast. The more traditional the theme, like the hunt or the Fourth of July, the more likely you are to find antiques that support it. Indeed, some people build collections around a theme and hold buffets to show off their finds. Though hunting is still a popular sport in England and elsewhere, a modern American hunt breakfast or dinner is largely a symbolic event celebrating the arrival of autumn. In the Berkshires, this is particularly appropriate, as the area is known for the beauty of its fall foliage. Because there are so many antique objects relating to the hunt and to the sporting life, it's easy to assemble enough to carry the theme: plates embellished with hunting scenes or individually painted pheasants, foxes, ducks,

The centerpiece at a luxurious breakfast at Blantyre is an egg and toast rack dating from 1860, with four egg cups, toast slots, and a dish to hold marmalade at the top. A silver-plate-and-glass 1870 butter dish, 1920s etched tumblers and fruit bowls, and 1800–1825 Irish Bright Cut flatware appoint the table, which has a lace runner in lieu of a tablecloth. The 1913 Minton plates make sprightly breakfast dishes.

At this lovely private home in the Berkshires, even the most ordinary bagels and lox can be turned into a special occasion when guests come. A sideboard conveniently positioned in the dining room is extremely useful, as guests can help themselves and then find a seat at the table, which eliminates the need for passing cumbersome or heavy platters.

or other game; horn-and-silver goblets; salt and pepper shakers in the form of silver birds; even tea-caddy ladles shaped like tiny riding hats. Other touches, such as serving cider in a silver tureen, using paisley shawls for table-cloths, substituting thistles for the usual floral decorations, and dotting the room with feathers, stuffed birds, and a few well-placed old bones, perfect the atmosphere.

"Fashions in china decoration are not fixed," Agnes Morton wrote in her 1894 *Etiquette.* "The fancy of the hour is constantly changing, but a matched set is eminently proper for the dinner table, leaving the 'harlequin' china for luncheons and teas. In the latter style, the aim is to have no two pieces alike in decoration, or at least, to permit an unlimited variety, a fashion that is very convenient when large quantities of dishes are liable to be needed." The harlequin style—a fancy way of saying mix and match—has never gone out of vogue, and is as useful and appealing today as when those sensible words were written. To create a harlequin style today, we might have something that links together all the china on the table, whether obvious or subtle—we might use plates that are all from the same period but of different patterns, or mix export napkin rings and cutlery with dishes that have an Oriental motif. Hostesses may even want to pick a decorative element, like porcelain Battersea boxes, and present each guest with his or her own mini-floral arrangement in the box. Actual harlequin tea and coffee sets, each piece having the same pattern painted in a different color, when you can find them, are especially appealing.

A buffet can make breakfast an event, especially if one uses an antique lace table runner, silver egg cruets and toast racks, beautiful engraved glasses for juice, and the best china. Another idea is to set the table as though for a sit-down meal and let everyone help themselves to the food from the sideboard. On another occasion, when an important breakfast might call for your best antique china, try contrasting the event with a casual lunch, at which you might serve bread on wooden boards, with knives placed directly on the table, and offer cutlery in well-used tool boxes (lined with paper, of course). Fill an old Staffordshire bowl with pasta salad and, instead of using plates, serve the salad in early-nineteenth-century soup bowls.

Inviting guests to your home after a concert or performance for a dessert buffet is a wonderful way to cap off the evening. It's also a fairly simple and inexpensive way to entertain. Desserts can be made or bought ahead of time and arranged on the sideboard. Coffee, served in pretty demitasses, or after-dinner cordials complement most any sweets, which you can serve on a highly decorative dessert set, perhaps one with gold and pink luster. And then, plate in hand, settle back against the cushions and enjoy the crackling of the fire as darkness gathers in the distance.

This delicate 1880s glass set serves melon balls as well as wine. Hand-painted Limoges fish plates from M. Redon and an ivory-handled fish knife match the menu. The George Adams sterling silver King's Husk flatware dates from 1843 to 1875.

A George III 1810 punch-bowl crafted by Paul Storr overflows with bagels, and the smoked salmon glistens in a meat dish, also made in 1810 by the famed English silversmith. The fish platter matches the plates on the table. Odd serving pieces, like this wide-pronged meat fork, can always be given a new purpose.

This dessert buffet evokes the feeling of another era, when the young set returned after a ball or a night at the Casino in Stockbridge to sup on cakes. Two eighteenth-century knife boxes and 1860s cut-glass candelabra flank this gorgeous spread at Naumkeag. The cups and saucers are an attractive silver and yellow lustreware dating from 1800.

Far right: A wedding at Wheatleigh blends gold-and-white china from a mix of 1813 Minton, 1890 Wedgwood, and 1900 Limoges patterns. A round Sheffield tray supports the wedding cake, with 1862 dessert forks alongside. Silver candlesticks hold flowers. Left: The bride's veil envelops a gold-rimmed champagne glass and a basket filled with rice cones perched on an elegant gilt chair.

An English silver-plated cake basket dating from 1880–1900 cradles napkins with commemorative bands.

Certain events require extra-special consideration. In the hierarchy of important occasions, golden anniversaries, half-century birthdays, and the like are pretty close to the top, but weddings reign supreme. Nothing compares with the mixture of solemnity and joyfulness and the desire to make the day especially memorable that characterize weddings. (In ancient societies, before there were certificates or licenses, the feast that celebrated a marriage had to be so remarkable that it would be remembered by all who attended.) There are hundreds of different ways to handle a wedding, but more than anything it should express romance. If you're going the route of the proper white wedding, play up its old-fashionedness. The four-tiered cake belongs on a round silver platter, a tray of gold-rimmed Champagne glasses to one side and a large silver cake knife and fork to the other. A mixture of gold-and-white patterned plates might span the table, while napkins fill silver cake baskets. Daintily twisted cones of rice might rest in another cake basket, while lush bouquets of flowers complete the picture.

ON AUGUST 9, 1850, A GROUP OF LITERARY BERK-

SHIRES NEIGHBORS THAT INCLUDED HERMAN

MELVILLE AND NATHANIEL HAWTHORNE CLIMBED

MONUMENT MOUNTAIN. HAWTHORNE'S EDITOR,

JAMES FIELD, WORE PATENT-LEATHER SHOES, AND

OLIVER WENDELL HOLMES CARRIED UP CHAMPAGNE

IN HIS DOCTOR'S BAG. RAIN SHOWERS GREETED THE

TROOP AT THE PEAK, AND HAWTHORNE AND

A L F R E S C O

MELVILLE, WHO MET FOR THE FIRST TIME ON THE

JAUNT, TOOK SHELTER TOGETHER BEHIND A ROCK,

KINDLING AN INTENSE FRIENDSHIP. IT WAS UNDOUBT-

EDLY NOT THE FIRST BERKSHIRES PICNIC—MELVILLE'S

GOOD FRIEND AND NEIGHBOR SARAH MOREWOOD

WAS NOT DUBBED "FAIRY BELT, PRINCESS OF PIC NIC"

FOR NOTHING—BUT IT'S PROBABLY ONE OF THE

MOST CELEBRATED: EVERY AUGUST, HIKERS RETRACE

THE ROUTE OF THAT ILLUSTRIOUS ENSEMBLE,

Previous pages and above: An eight-course banquet for one on the great lawn of Belle-fontaine, the marble mansion formerly owned by Giraud Foster and now the Canyon Ranch spa, is accompanied by music from students at Tanglewood, an ebonized torchiere, and an enormous ornate champagne bucket. Eleven pieces of silver in Gorham's Chantilly pattern and three goblets, one of sterling silver, make up the place setting for the meal. The Ashworth ironstone plates dating from 1850–1870, in an impressive Oriental pattern, have a suitably solemn quality for this gourmet's repast.

Right: Numerous dinner accessories evolved in the second half of the nineteenth century to celebrate the act of dining. Menu holders came into vogue to document ever-more-elaborate meals.

ALFRESCO

Clear Soup, custard garnish
Barley Cream Soup

Red Mullet, Italian sauce
Lamb's Sweetbread in Cases

Green Peas, French style
Fried Potatoes
Roast Chicken, watercress garnish

Celery and Pimento Salad

Vanilla Soufflé
Strawberry Open Tart
Savoury Sardine Croustades

Cheese

climbing to the top with the necessary provisions, such as champagne in a doctor's bag and the requisite reading, and today picnics of all kinds are as much a part of life in the Berkshires as ever. The numerous theaters, Tanglewood, and the glorious vistas of the mountains provide perfect venues for outdoor dining. From a simple pre-show supper on the grass to an elaborate sit-down dinner under the stars, eating alfresco is one of the best ways to enjoy the summer.

Picnics are license for creativity, a chance to experiment in ways you never would indoors. Remember that nature tends to overwhelm subtle colors, so consider using some really bright, bold linens and table accessories. Use the most colorful china you can find: flow blue, the brightest of the blue-and-whites; hand-painted Gaudy Welsh, with its floral decorations in cobalt blue, red, and copper luster; or just about any vivid garden-floral china.

Picnics originated in the eighteenth century as a kind of potluck meal, with each guest bringing a portion of the edibles. Only later, in the nineteenth century, did they become associated specifically with dining outdoors. The Victorians embraced the picnic as a reprieve from their customary formality. "The great charm of this social device," according to an 1869 magazine editorial, "is undoubtedly the freedom it affords. It is to eat, to chat, to lie, to sit, to talk, to walk, with something of the unconstraint of primitive life." The Victorians, increasingly seduced by the comforts of industrialization, revered nature with an intense nostalgia but came prepared for it as if they were going into the jungle. Mrs. Beeton, never one to be caught off guard, recommends, after a monstrous list of food, things "not to be forgotten": "a stick of horseradish, a bottle of mint-sauce well corked, a bottle of salad dressing, a bottle of vinegar, made mustard, pepper, salt, good oil, and pounded sugar. If it can be managed, take a little ice. It is scarcely necessary to say that plates, tumblers, wine-glasses, knives, forks, and spoons, must not be forgotten; as also teacups and saucers, three or four teapots, some lump sugar, and milk, if this last-named article cannot be obtained in the neighborhood. Take three corkscrews. Beverages—three dozen quart bottles of ale, packed in hampers; ginger-beer, soda water, and lemonade, of each two dozen bottles; six bottles of sherry, six bottles of claret, Champagne, at discretion, and any other light wine that may be preferred, and two bottles of brandy. Water can usually be obtained; so it is useless to take it."

Picnics were day-long outings, often equipped to serve as many as forty both for lunch and for tea. In this era before paper plates and plastic cups, the glass, china, and silver were carefully wrapped, strapped, and packed in baskets and hampers. Special sets of dishes designed solely for picnicking did exist, but these were few and far between. More likely, a family would take their everyday or second-best set, or an assortment of odd pieces. Despite the thrill that came from roughing it, servants were an integral part of these excursions, setting up, discreetly disappearing, and then reappearing to clean up. In his autobiography, Frederick Vanderbilt Field recalled picnics in the children's playhouse at High Lawn, his grandparents' house in Lenox: "The picnic procedure never varied. In the middle of the afternoon preceding the outing, an observer would have seen the butler carrying a large tray of silverware, plates, and linen from the big house. Some time later, he would be followed by the 'fourth man' carrying cooking utensils, eggs, cream, salt and pepper. We participants would then gather at the appointed hour around the electric stove, and the picnic would get underway. An outstanding

Afternoon tea at Peirson Place is brightened by Gaudy Welsh, an inexpensive, cheerful, and naive bone china made in Staffordshire from the 1820s to the 1860s for export primarily to American markets. Following pages: A mix of old and new gives this eccentric picnic in front of an old silo behind an early colonial home its flavor: a handmade 1817 jacquard coverlet; new napkins; eighteenth-century Chinese red clay teapots, called Yi-hsing wares, whose small size and odd shapes greatly appealed to the Western market; 1840–1850 Staffordshire plates in the Quadruped pattern; new cutlery; old picnic baskets; and pressed-glass goblets for iced tea perched on an old soda box.

feature was that everyone was in a good humor. I wonder if that was not because we were, for a change, relatively on our own, away from the servants for a whole meal."

Today our outings, though not less enjoyable, are on a far simpler scale. A picnic should be a chance to savor being outdoors, not to worry about lugging enormous quantities of fragile antiques to a grassy nook. Be realistic—don't take precious glasses or china. Instead, bring along sturdy contemporary tumblers and some favorite everyday transferware plates, or odds and ends of old sets. These can be carefully packaged and safely carried in a wicker hamper. Picnic baskets, old and new, come in a variety of shapes, many with pockets and straps expressly designed for carrying crockery and flatware; it's also fun to give each person his or her own basket. Even old teapots can make the trip, provided they're well protected en route; they are useful for serving everything from hot tea to cool white wine. Giving an individual teapot to each member of the outing, serving on old blue-and-white export plates, or bringing along silver grape shears

will give a sense of elegance and permanence to the meal and make it far more memorable. Sandwiches generally provide the bulk of picnic fare, but you could liven up the ordinary

Down the garden path from the silo, a formal luncheon awaits in the rotunda. The ribbon pattern on the napkins and the crisp linen tablecloth echo the twining vine on the column. A simple color scheme of red and green keeps this dainty table setting very fresh—antique cranberry and clear glasses, hand-painted dessert plates, and 1820 Coalport cups and saucers. Note the grooved ivory handles on the flatware.

with some true Victorian fillings— edible violets, rose petals, or nasturtiums. One 1893 cookbook suggested tying up each crustless sandwich with ribbon—red for tongue sandwiches, pink for ham, light yellow for

The invention in 1828 of machines that pressed glass into molds revolutionized glass production and design. Two unusual examples are this intricately rendered cake stand on wheels and the "broken column" dish, ideally suited for bananas.

A garden party can occur at any hour, but one at tea time is particularly pleasant. At Peirson Place, the service is an 1830 pink lustreware, accompanied by mother-of-pearl cake forks, an embellished cake knife, and a wide 1920 cake server. The American pressed-glass cake stands were made between 1850 and 1890.

chicken, and lily white for bread and butter. "Sandwiches should always be wrapped neatly in white tis-
sue-paper and tied with narrow ribbon. The extra care
and expense are trifling, and are repaid by the dainti-
ness of the result."

While picnicking suggests a studied informality, dining alfresco deserves the most proper attention. Pliny
the Elder, describing a meal at his Tuscan villa, wrote
how water flowed into "a fine, polished marble basin, so
artfully contrived that it is always full without ever
overflowing. When I sup here this basin serves for a
table, the largest sort of dishes being placed around the
margin, while the smaller ones swim about in the form
of little vessels and waterfowls." Though even the Berkshires cottagers probably didn't spoon their baked
Alaska from floating bowls, most of the grand houses
had sheltered porches and gardens, equipped with
fountains, in which to enjoy dignified lunches while
"swimming" in what Henry James described as "a bath

of beauty." At Brookhurst, designed by Ogden Codman, Gouverneur Newbold
Morris often invited his first cousin and neighbor Edith Wharton and other
friends to dine out-of-doors, while at Naumkeag, Miss Mabel Choate's favorite
form of entertaining was luncheon under the shingled canopy, with baby peas
and carrots from the greenhouses, musicales in renowned landscape designer
Fletcher Steele's serpentine gardens, and lingering strolls on the linden walk.
Mrs. deHeredia served tea on the lawn at Wheatleigh every Sunday afternoon
at 5:00 during the season, and outdoor bake sales, with white linen tablecloths
flapping in the breeze and a press of cake stands, compotes, sweetmeat dishes,
doughnut stands, loaf trays, and their colorful contents, were, then as now, a
favorite fund-raising activity. Today many of the old houses that have become
museums still have outdoor fund raisers.

*A late-nineteenth-cen-
tury bake sale, still a
favorite American fund
raiser, might have
included a panoramic
assortment of pressed-
glass patterns in com-
potes, cake stands, pie
plates, doughnut stands,
sweetmeat dishes, and
covered fruit dishes.*

Previous pages: Just one or two unusual touches can make a casual meal special. White Cauldon plates dating from the 1880s decorated with yellow flowers pick up the color scheme at luncheon on the terrace of this private home near Tanglewood. At right, a breakfast on the balcony of another home features fruit with an exquisite set of gilded spoons, forks, and a berry serving spoon. The balcony overlooks a garden maze recently planted by the owner, a landscape architect, for her children.

Built in the 1850s, this gazebo at Peirson Place is the site of a celebratory summer meal. The dramatic moire chintz tablecloth brings out the decoration on the turn-of-the-century Royal Worcester plates, which in turn complement the 1860 green thumb-molded English wine goblets. Mother-of-pearl-handled fruit knives and forks are ready for the second course.

Singular, provocative objects, such as a French frosted glass candlestick in the form of a woman and unusual silver condiment servers, capture a fantastical air appropriate to the vivid colors and drama of the twilight garden setting.

In addition, Chesterwood has outdoor exhibitions of contemporary art. Naumkeag recreates the late-afternoon musicales of an earlier era under its shingled eaves, with singers—dressed in starched white blouses and flowing skirts—singing from sheet music almost a century old.

Many nineteenth-century families, embracing the prevailing fashion for the picturesque, built gazebos or garden houses, some thatched with moss, others bedecked with Gothic turrets and arches. Filled with portable wicker or wooden "fancy" chairs, or heavy cast- or wrought-iron furniture, these follies constituted the visual focal point of the garden and provided an escape from some of the heat of indoors. Gazebos have lost none of their charm and can be delightful outdoor eating areas. Walled gardens and clearings underneath the trees are also enchanting. But even without these, there are so many modern conveniences (large white canvas beach umbrellas, lamps, citronella candles and torches to keep bugs away) that eating outdoors on golden afternoons and cool starry nights can be as elegant as any nineteenth-century gala affair.

THERE IS NO MOMENT QUITE LIKE THE FIVE MINUTES

OR SO BEFORE THE GUESTS ARRIVE AND A DINNER PARTY

BEGINS. THE HOUSE IS PRISTINE, THE KITCHEN IS BRIM-

MING WITH DELIGHTS, AND THE DINING TABLE IS SET—

I ALWAYS TAKE A MINUTE TO ENJOY THE FRESH CLEAN

CLOTH, THE SPARKLING SILVER, CHINA, AND GLASS AT

EACH PLACE, THE CRISP NAPKINS, THE FRAGRANT FLOW-

ERS. THE PARTY WILL FLOURISH WITH ANIMATED CON-

VERSATION, LAUGHTER, AND DELICIOUS FOOD, BUT AT

NO OTHER TIME WILL THE DINING ROOM BE SO PURELY

BEAUTIFUL. THEN I CHECK THAT THERE'S WATER IN THE

DRINKING GLASSES, LIGHT THE CANDLES ON THE TABLE

AND MANTELPIECE, AND LET THE EVENING BEGIN.

THE DINING ROOM

NO OTHER ROOM IS LIKE THE DINING ROOM OR

HOLDS AS MANY CONCENTRATED MEMORIES OF FAM-

ILY AND FRIENDS—IT'S THE HEART OF FAMILY LIFE,

WHERE ALL THE IMPORTANT CELEBRATIONS AND

holidays take place. And no other room glows like the dining room dressed for a party. Yet the need for a dining room often comes to people later in life. Most young families feel they can make do without one, viewing a dining room as unpractical, a waste of much-needed space, or too intimidating. It's true that dining room furniture represents probably the biggest furniture purchase a couple will make, and it can be the hardest room in the house to decorate, precisely because it is the most steeped in tradition. But most younger couples use rustic versions of traditional dining-room features, perhaps substituting a blue painted cabinet for a mahogany sideboard or a long harvest table for a Georgian one. A dining room makes a meal special the way nothing else can, even if the table is an old one, covered with a pretty cloth. One can argue that dining rooms are as much a state of mind as a real place, and that a festive feeling can be achieved as easily at the kitchen table or in an open loft, but for those who have dining rooms—use

Previous pages: Dining in the Berkshires is steeped in history. At The Mount, an ornate 1752–1789 candelabrum, crafted by John Cafe and William Pitts, a silver champagne bucket, delicate glasses, a handmade Italian lace tablecloth, and an antique Aubusson car-

pet set the stage for a dramatic event. Below and right: Old-fashioned ladderback chairs give Arrowhead a more homey feel. This one belonged to the parsonage of the Reverend Thomas Allen, the "Fighting Parson" of Pittsfield, and dates between 1775 and 1780.

and enjoy them! Don't save them only for holiday dinners.

The dining room moved all over the house before it settled down in the spot we are accustomed to, near the kitchen and pantry. During the Middle Ages and well beyond, families ate in the kitchen or great hall, with furniture that fulfilled a multitude of uses: trestle tables that could be dismantled when not in use; settles that acted as both bench and chest, with high backs to guard against drafts; tables that became chairs when you flipped up the top; and refectory-type tables that could hide long, low benches underneath. In the eighteenth century, wealthy families in Europe and America began building houses with separate spaces for dining, and by the mid-nineteenth century dining rooms had become firmly established as an architectural feature in middle-class homes. But even then, these rooms were often used in many ways.

The breakfast table at Arrowhead on which Herman Melville penned Moby Dick *is a handsome English* pedestal-base tilt-top model, designed to flip up for easier storage.

Drop-leaf tables with D-ends, like this Hepplewhite mahogany table from the 1700s, evolved in the second half of the eighteenth century. Versatile and attractive (note the Marlborough legs), the ends can form two separate side tables or a round table for small gatherings, the center section can be pushed against the wall as a buffet, or, as at right, all three together can make a long oval. The only drawback to these tables are the numerous legs.

The pedestal base, associated with the American furniture designer Duncan Phyfe and others, became popular from the late 1700s to the early 1900s, and remains a highly sought after style today because of the maximum leg space it provides for the comfort of diners. This Grecian-style mahogany table has scroll feet.

A tasteful mix of antiques decorates this private dining room. The Queen Anne chairs, characterized by a vase-shaped splat and cabriole legs, set off a mahogany 1718–1779 Chippendale drop-leaf table.

In addition to a black walnut extension table and six black walnut chairs with cane seats, one typical 1853 American dining room also contained a mahogany sofa, two rockers, a clock, a stove, a spittoon, and a cherry tea table, and the room served also as a sitting room.

In his 1793 guide for cabinetmakers, the English designer Thomas Sheraton wrote, "The general style of furnishing a dining parlour should be in substantial and useful things, avoiding trifling ornaments and unnecessary decorations. The pillars are emblematic of the use we make of these rooms, in which we eat the principal meal for nature's support. The furniture, without exception, is of mahogany, as being the most suitable for such apartments." This sentiment was reflected in the development of the dark, somber dining room so characteristic of the Victorian era, paneled with heavy wood or hung with leather and situated to give a northern exposure, suitable to the grave purpose of dining. Earlier (eighteenth-century) dining parlors, particularly Continental ones, were decorated with exotic painted motifs on the ceiling and had light-colored walls. This look tends to be much more congenial to today's tastes, though popular Victorian wall decorations—still lifes of fruit bursting with ripeness and decay, and game and fish trussed up on hooks—are still favored today.

Proper dining-room tables, with a

rectangular top on solid, bulbous legs joined by a floor stretcher, date from the middle of the sixteenth century. Toward the end of the seventeenth century, the prevalent forms were round or oval gateleg tables in walnut or maple, with six or eight legs and side flaps. The extra legs, connected at the top and bottom by stretchers, swing out like a gate to support the flaps. Georgian tables of about 1720–60 were also oval or round, but had cabriole legs connected only at the top that supported the drop leaves. A popular variation, the so-called D-shape drop-leaf table, consists of a center table with two oblong drop leaves at the sides and two separate semicircular tables at the ends, usually with drop leaves as well. These early extension tables were made in every style, from simple country to ornately carved Grecian, with scroll feet or delicately painted floral swags in the style of contemporary porcelain. The Chippendale period of the mid-eighteenth

century ushered in smaller drop-leaf and Pembroke tables, elegant tables suitable for a lady or gentleman to breakfast on that were usually placed against the wall or between two windows when not in use. In the late 1700s and early 1800s, the work of such craftsmen as Duncan Phyfe popularized the pedestal-base table, which provided the maximum amount of leg space for the comfort of diners. One-piece extension tables, with extra leaves for extra guests, were but a short step away, and in the 1850s one newspaper writer described the possible shapes for dining tables as "the square, the oblong, the oval, the round, and the extension table, all of which are approved, though the three latter are esteemed the most elegant."

Put together with wit, style, and minimal expense, this eclectic dining room combines rustic painted Hitchcock chairs, a rustic drop-leaf table, and more formal Federal accessories.

The pedestal-base style has remained the most popular shape in dining tables to this day, sometimes to the neglect of drop-leaf and gateleg models. But while pedestal-base mahogany tables look the part for the grand art of dining, drop-leaf and gateleg tables are perhaps more suitable for everyday or intimate occasions. (They also tend to be proportionately less expensive.) If your heart is set on a mahogany pedestal table, consider one of the superbly crafted examples from the 1910s and 1920s, which can be a very good buy; they don't have the cachet of older pieces, but they are better made and less expensive than comparable tables being produced today, and have the patina of age.

Other tables still useful in the dining room are pier tables, originally meant, according to Sheraton, "merely for ornament under a [looking] glass," or mirror. They function well as side tables during a dinner party, and some, called hunt boards, made with marble tops, serve as drinks tables. In her 1878 book, *The Dining Room*, Mrs. Loftie recommended small portable tables for serving that "may be moved near to the fire in winter or into the bow window in summer." Tea tables came in with the drinking of tea, but were not made in quantity until it became fashionable to invite friends home for tea rather than to sip it in public tea gardens. Chippendale offered various designs for "china tables," generally oblong with a raised rim and an irregular edge to accommodate the china tea set. Some of these tea tables had removable trays. Another form was the tripod-base tea table, often with a tilting top and a "bird cage" device that allowed the top to turn. When the table was not in use, it could be folded up and tucked out of the way. A familiar circular example is today called the "piecrust" table, a pedestal-base table whose top has a scalloped or wavy-edged rim.

As trestle tables and straightforward rectangular tables gave way to round and oval shapes, benches and stools gave way to chairs. Chairs for the dining room demanded special consideration. They had to be sturdy, lightweight, comfortable for long hours, and easily cleaned. A journalist advising aspiring hostesses in the 1850s wrote, "Let her have chairs with spring seats and spring backs, quite unlike ordinary dinner chairs" (good advice, though few people followed it). Edith Wharton, in her and Ogden Codman's book, *The Decoration of Houses*, described her favorite dining chairs, those from the eighteenth century, which, "whether cane seated or upholstered, were invariably made with wide deep seats, so that the long banquets of the day might be endured without constraint or fatigue; while the backs were low and narrow, in order not to interfere with the service of the table." The seats tended to be cane or leather, and, by the nineteenth century, they were sold in sets of anywhere from six to twenty-four. The plentiful maple, yellow pine, and soft white pine were the woods typically used in New England. The fruit woods (cherry, apple, and pear), walnut, and mahogany were reserved for finer pieces.

Today we mix and match, and our dining table might come from one era and our chairs from another. Furthermore, it's much easier to find chairs in groups of two, three, four, or even six, rather than eight, ten, or twelve, so putting together a mixed set is sensible and economical. Find chairs that are of the same period if not the same style, or are of the same size or wood. Some people choose chairs that are entirely different from one another. This creates a powerful look, but if you do not have a collection of great examples it may draw more attention than you wish to that feature of the dining room.

*Right: Edith Wharton
and Ogden Codman's
The Decoration of
Houses was responsible
for sweeping away
heavy Victorian excess
and bringing back
classical styles. Pho-
tographed in the great
hall at The Mount, this
historical range of
chairs includes, clock-
wise from bottom left, a
rosewood Hepplewhite-
style shell-back arm-
chair; an 1800–1820
American mahogany
empire chair; an ornate
nineteenth-century
Queen Anne-style chair;
a 1780 Thomas Chip-
pendale Gansevoort
chair, made for General
Peter Gansevoort; an
1876 mahogany chair in
the Chinese Chippen-
dale style; a 1795 Shera-
ton-style American
Federal mahogany
chair; and, in the center,
an 1820–1830 side chair
with a mahogany
veneer.*

*Previous page: A photo
of the underside shows
the mechanism for
expanding a Regency
double pedestal base
table, still one of the
most popular table
forms, and the graceful
lines of American
Federal chairs.*

Side tables with drawers and cabinets for use in the dining room developed in the last quarter of the eighteenth century. This early classic Irish mahogany sideboard has a railing around the edge.

This unusual American sideboard is both storage unit and desk and could fulfill a number of uses in a house that can't afford to devote a room solely to dining. Blue-and-white delftware always looks handsome on the rich surfaces of old wood.

A tall Federal side cupboard is an elegant piece of furniture, though more appropriate, perhaps, for storing than for serving.

An English Sheraton-period sideboard has an array of drawers and cupboards, including sliding doors, and is a perfect height on which to place serving dishes.

The bird-cage device on this tripod-based tilt-top eighteenth-century mahogany tea table allows the surface to revolve as well as to flip up for easier storage. Right: Muffin or cake stands were common accompaniments at Victorian teas. Simple, three-tiered mahogany versions like this one could stand chairside, while smaller silver examples could perch right on the table.

later sold, since the copies are obviously not antiques.

Chairs are one category of furniture you can try before you buy, so consider style and comfort carefully. Ladderback chairs first appeared during the reign of William and Mary (1689–1702), and their popularity has endured since then. With turned posts, flat and sometimes shaped splats, and rush, cane, or slatted seats, they ranged in look from the very rustic to the supremely ornamental. The Queen Anne chair, a baroque style introduced about 1720, is characterized by cabriole legs, a vase-shaped splat, a yoke-shaped crest rail, and pad or slipper feet. Often, it was decorated with carved shell ornaments. Chippendale, the name given to the rococo style of the second half of the eighteenth century, was named as much for the cabinetmaker himself as for the style he introduced via his *The Gentleman and Cabinetmaker's Director,* first published in 1754. The distinguishing features are ornate carving, Gothic and chinoiserie design elements, C and S scrolls, cabriole legs, pierced splats, and ball-and-claw feet. The Federal period in America, also known

Many people buy sets of six and have differing host and hostess chairs, usually with arms and often upholstered. Another idea is to have chairs made to match an existing set; this is less expensive than it might appear, but could devalue the set if the chairs are

as Sheraton or Hepplewhite after the two great English designers of the day, featured neoclassical designs that were lighter, thinner, and more planar than in previous pieces. Contrasting colored veneers provided bold color effects, as did elegant painting. The period, which lasted from 1790 to 1815, produced many different types of chairs, including the splat back, vase or shield back, square back, oval back, heart back, scroll back, and lyre back.

Regency is an English term used to describe neoclassical furniture made during the first forty years of the nineteenth century, or, more precisely, during the regency of George, Prince of Wales (1811–20), and his reign as George IV (1820–30). Georgian, on the other hand, refers to the reigns of the second and third Georges and is divided into early (1729–65) and late (1765–1820) periods; it describes a more general eighteenth-century style. Windsor chairs, invented about 1750, had interchangeable parts and were therefore relatively inexpensive to make. These chairs, which have spindle backs and plank seats, are still much favored; look for early painted

examples, usually dark green or black, or later examples with fine finishes.

Nineteenth-century craftsmen borrowed from every phase of history when adorning their furniture. From 1805 to 1850, the Empire and Grecian styles, influenced by the archaeological finds of the Napoleonic era, dominated the decorative arts. Craftsmen, led by the workshop of Duncan Phyfe, adapted the klismos chair form, with a curved back that "hugs" the diner, and decorated every surface with scrolls, reeding, gilt-bronze ornaments such as eagles and dolphins, and other classical motifs. The Gothic revival superseded

that, drawing on ecclesiastical decorative elements such as arches, crockets, and quatrefoils. The French period, a reinterpretation of eighteenth-century rococo, saw furnishings in rosewood, mahogany, and black walnut with gilding and forms shaped by steam bending and lamination. The Renaissance revival, at its height between 1865 and 1880, drew on a variety of historical influences, including Louis XIV. These chairs and other objects, often highlighted with incised gilding, light-colored burl veneers, and marquetry, feature gilt and porcelain ornaments, Roman medallions, palmettes, urns, rondels, columns, masks, and other architectural devices from the ancient world. "Fancy" chairs (an improvement on the traditional Windsor form) were lightweight, mass-produced chairs with painted, grained, stenciled, and gilded finishes, cane or rush seats, and turned legs and stiles. The Hitchcock shop in Connecticut is famous for such chairs, but there were many small manufacturers that produced them.

By about 1880 a reaction to the excesses of the French-inspired styles had set in. Charles Locke Eastlake's *Hints on Household Taste* called for a

design reform, encouraging simple, rectilinear shapes, shallow relief carving, turned spindles, and leather upholstery. This new style was particularly suited to the dining room, being easy to clean, chaste, and in keeping with family values. (Today, many of us would find this style as heavy as that of some of the other periods.) Colonial revival, which hit all areas of the decorative arts in the last quarter of the nineteenth century—and is still current in furniture—looked back to eighteenth-century forms and styles. Queen Anne furniture was especially popular, but most colonial revival pieces were reinterpretations of earlier styles rather than authentic reproductions, until Wallace Nutting introduced the idea of historical accuracy in the 1920s and 1930s.

Another important feature of the dining room was the sideboard. This had been developed in the last part of the eighteenth century, usually with two deep lead- or baize-lined drawers for holding bottles of wine or china. The lead-lined drawers could also hold water to wash wine glasses, a practice that can't have been very healthy. On the other hand, as Shera-

ton explained in 1785, some sideboards "are often made without drawers of any sort, having simply a rail a little ornamented, and pedestals with vases at each end . . . . One pedestal is used as a plate warmer, and is lined with tin; the other as a pot-cupboard, and sometimes it contains a cellarette for wine. The vases are used for water for the use of the butler, and sometimes as knife-cases . . . ." (The pot-cupboard held a chamber pot for after-dinner use by gentlemen so inclined.) Other favorite pieces were marble-topped or mahogany consoles, which were side tables attached to the wall by brackets.

By the mid-nineteenth century, the sideboard had adopted the form of a medieval cupboard (also called a court cupboard, buffet by the French, or credenza by the Italians), with doors below and shelves above for displaying china. Heavily carved, these pieces were often decorated with ormolu, inlaid porcelain plaques, or marquetry panels. Later, the upper shelves sometimes had mirrored backs and were enclosed with glass doors. "The sideboard is always enormous and unwieldy, and upon it are somewhat set

A legacy of the traditional preciousness of Chinese porcelain, china cabinets—initially glass-fronted cabinets sitting on a table top—were developed to store, protect, and display a family's prized collection. This grand lacquered cabinet holds a 1938 Minton pattern.

A cellarette, a chest made for storing wine, typically held a dozen bottles. Many are Federal in style, sometimes with inlaid decoration.

the affections and ambitions of the family," an American visiting an English dining room in 1881 wrote. "It is quite usually the most expensive piece of furniture in the house, and it is not only very big, very high, very wide, and very long, but it is elaborately carved and ornamented with brass trimmings. It is, in some sense, the symbol of hospitality. The biscuit box is always standing upon it, and the decanters of wine and spirits are always at hand." As sideboards became more and more massive, dining rooms were more often built with a special niche meant to contain the piece and alleviate congestion around the table. Maria Parloa described the function of a sideboard in an 1892 *Ladies Home Journal:* "The drawers are for the silver and cutlery, the closets for wines, if they be used, and often for such things as preserved ginger, confectionery, cut sugar, and indeed, any of the many little things that one likes to have in the dining room, yet out of sight. The water pitcher and other silver and pretty bits of china can be placed on the sideboard. Cracker jar and fruit dish also belong there. At dinner time the dessert dishes are usually arranged upon it."

Corner cupboards, popular in American homes from colonial days onward, have a closed cupboard below and shelves, with glass or solid doors, above. This one houses a collection of treen—biscuit barrels with silver handles, a 1760 George III egg cruet, and variously sized salt dishes.

*Lighting is most impor-
tant in the dining room.
Candles are the tradi-
tional method and are
still used today, whether
wax or electric. This
Swedish glass chande-
lier forms a cascade of
shimmering light.
Following pages, right:
Side tables with marble
tops can be very useful
during a dinner party,
providing a safe surface
for drinks and hot
dishes. An 1830 Ameri-
can Duncan Phyfe table
sports 1810 French
bronze Dore cande-
labra. Below is an
English 1820 mahogany
decanter chest.*

Delicately wrought flowers, figures, and gilded decoration ornament this porcelain Meissen chandelier, giving the room a very romantic feel.

Wall sconces are often used in conjunction with mirrors to further intensify the light from the flame.

Other serving pieces included corner cupboards, often built into the corner of a room, which sometimes had closed cabinets down below and open shelves above; dressers, with cupboards below for storage and open shelves above for display; and lazy Susans in wood or silver, very much like the ones we use today, that spun condiments on the sideboard or table. China cabinets, a legacy of the traditional preciousness of Chinese porcelain, were developed to store, protect, and display a family's prize collection. Generally these had a table base and a glassed-in cabinet top; sometimes there was a small locking drawer as well. By the late 1800s, the form had become a freestanding cabinet, with rounded glass sides, a mirrored back, and a glass door, perched on low cabriole legs and having several glass shelves. It served as an adjunct to the sideboard for storing sets of cut glass, porcelain, or fancy earthenware. In addition to tea caddies, there were several small wooden boxes made for storage. A cellarette, or *garde de vin*, often in elegant Federal style with decorative inlays, held a dozen wine bottles. Knife cases and boxes with hinged lids held sets of table knives and were generally placed on the sideboard. Today, though a sideboard can be one of the most useful elements in the dining room, there are storage and serving alternatives that are a little less formal. Any kind of long shelf, table, or even trolley will work well for holding serving dishes, salad bowl, and so forth.

However you furnish your dining room, with whatever blend of old and new, it won't be complete without proper lighting. The most important thing to keep in mind is that the color of the walls and the lighting should be soft and flattering to people's faces—after all, it's a place where we're sitting in proximity with our neighbors for hours at a time. Even though some turn-of-the-century cottagers employed electric fixtures in their dining rooms—like electric-power pioneer George Westinghouse's quilted ceiling and mosaic of unshaded light bulbs at Erskine Park—candlesticks and chandeliers were the preferred form of lighting. "For the dining table, even in the electrically lighted house, nothing better than candles, carefully shaded, has ever been found," Oliver Coleman observed in *Successful Houses* in 1902. "A lamp is clumsy and obstructs the view, while overhead lighting usually gets in the eyes. Furthermore, the candles, in their silver sticks with their small colored shades, are in themselves a charming decoration." The candle shades Coleman mentions have experienced something of a revival, being practical and decorative, and unique in that they can be used over lighted candles.

Candlesticks come in everything from tin, wood, and simple redware to glass, brass, porcelain, and silver, or a mixture of materials. The terminology can be confusing: a candelabrum holds more than one candle, while candelabra refers to more than one candelabrum. Just to make it difficult, a girandole consists of a candelabrum, usually brass with a gilt finish on a marble base and cut-glass prisms hanging from the ornaments under the sockets, flanked by a freestanding pair of candlesticks on either side. Highly ornate, girandoles took pride of place more often on the mantelpiece than the table. Cut-glass chandeliers symbolize gracious dining, with their layers of refractive brilliance, but wall sconces offer a beautiful subtle light, either alone or, as in days of yore, in conjunction with mirrors.

THERE'S NOTHING LIKE THE FEEL OF AN OLD-

FASHIONED PANTRY—THE WELL-WORN WOOD, THE

DIM LIGHT, THE STACKS OF PLATES AND ROWS OF

CUPS BEHIND GLASS. THE PANTRY, A PRIVATE AND

SECLUDED PLACE FILLED WITH SECRETS IN ITS CABI-

NETS AND TREASURES IN ITS DRAWERS, BEARS WIT-

THE PANTRY

NESS TO YEARS OF FAMILY HISTORY. CHINA CLOSETS

FITTED WITH SHELVES FIRST BEGAN TO APPEAR IN

HOUSE LAYOUTS ABOUT 1800, AND FULL-FLEDGED

PANTRIES WITH SINKS BEGAN APPEARING IN WEALTHY

HOMES FIFTY YEARS LATER.

LATE-VICTORIAN ARCHITECTS AND THEIR CLIENTS

DELIGHTED IN THE SPECIALIZATION OF ROOM FUNC-

TIONS AS MUCH AS OF OBJECTS. UNFORTUNATELY,

THIS FONDNESS, PARTICULARLY IN THE SERVANTS'

WING, RESULTED IN LONG DARK CORRIDORS BE-

TWEEN ROWS OF NUMEROUS TINY CHAMBERS AND

Previous pages: The pantry at Naumkeag is a cool, beautifully pan-elled room with plenty of space to attend to behind-the-scenes activi-ties like clearing the breakfast trays.
Left and below right: A built-in sideboard at Blantyre, part of the original dining room, holds a huge floral arrangement prepared in the adjacent pantry.

closets. In addition to the kitchen, grand Victorian country houses included a scullery for washing and storing china and glassware, a pantry, meat larder, game larder, fish larder, dairy and dairy scullery, a knife room, a butler's pantry with an adja-cent silver safe and silver scullery, a housekeeper's room, and a still room, in which cakes were baked. Though nineteenth-century builders made the division of culinary labors into an art form, many of these rooms were based on medieval traditions. The pantry, from the Italian *panetteria*, meaning bakery, generally stocked dry foods, staple ingredients like sugar and flour, jars of pickles and preserves, and, after the mid-nineteenth century, cans. The larder, on the other hand, though today we use the term interchangeably with pantry, stored meat and other perishables. The scullery referred originally to a board for washing and drying eating utensils, and came over time to mean the whole room or area of the kitchen equipped with storage closets, vast sinks for washing up, and the unfortunates whose job it was to clean up after meals. (Who can forget poor Ruby in the television series *Upstairs, Downstairs?*) Most American houses were on a simpler scale, but many contained at least a pantry, which often combined all of these functions. In houses built today, of course, refrigerators serve as larders, kitchen cabinets as pantries, and sinks as sculleries.

Still, it's necessary to have a place to store china, glass, and silver, and the pantry today has taken on that role, almost to the exclusion of keeping food. If you can blend attractiveness with practicality, so much the better. Glassed-in cabinets are a favorite, being easy to see through and good-looking. If you don't have a full-fledged pantry or space to create one, you might consider converting a closet into a pantry, with felt-lined shelves and drawers for china and silver.

Wherever you decide to put your things, there are several important points to remember. Don't overcrowd, even though it's tempting. Glass rims shouldn't touch and there should be plenty of space between china objects. Don't stack different sizes of plates on top of each other, especially if you are constantly reaching for the bottom ones. If the plates are very precious, you might want to put a paper napkin or a piece of cloth or felt between them. Always make sure your tableware is thoroughly dry before you put it away. Many old cabinets possess hooks for hanging cups; it's acceptable to use these as long as you are careful about not nicking the cup handles. Some people keep their silver in a safe, but if you use yours often, you might prefer to keep it in a closet or cabinet furnished with a strong lock that you can turn when you are away.

The pantry's placement often makes it handy for a stop between kitchen and dining-room table, to add last-minute preparations to a platter, light the candles on the birthday cake, or adjust the garnish atop the roast. But pantries can also be the staging area for grander achievements. As many pantries are equipped with a deep sink, they can be the best place to arrange flowers, especially if you keep your vases and vessels in one of the cabinets. The proximity of your glass and china holdings should inspire you to try new combinations. I've had luck with just about everything from traditional silver Victorian nosegay holders to horn funnels, cordial glasses, and candlesticks. Filled with vibrant colors, everyday items can take on new life at dinner parties. For the most formal occasion, you might prepare a more traditional centerpiece, such as roses in a silver Revere bowl.

When creating a floral concoction for the dining room, remember that the larger the arrangement, the easier it is to make. Put a sheet or piece of plastic on the floor or countertop to ease the cleanup and then select a container. Pitchers, tureens,

bowls, vases, and ewers all make good containers for large arrangements—as long as they're waterproof, of course. At the bottom of your vase, wrap a sheet of chicken wire around a block of Oasis (available at many florists and garden centers). The wire acts solely as a support and framework for the stalks, so you needn't be too precise about its shape. Then, simply stuff in the flowers of your choice—lilies, goldenrod, daisies, black-eyed Susans, cosmos, ferns, and astilbe all make long-lasting displays—and add water. Chances are the flowers will look pretty good almost at random, and with a tug here and a fluff there, you'll have perfection.

Left: Pantries, like this one in a private home in the Berkshires, make ideal spots for arranging flowers, with water nearby and interesting containers in view. Three Imari-patterned 1860 Mason's ironstone pitchers in various sizes make a wonderful centerpiece, right, as does a more exotic arrangement in an ornate tea urn, above.
Following pages: One hundred years of china history are stored in the wide glassed-in shelves of this old-fashioned pantry.

Medium and small arrangements, unless it's a single perfect rose in a bud vase, are surprisingly more difficult. While long-stemmed, large-blossomed, leafy flowers somehow always arrange themselves in a pleasing formation, it seems necessary to fuss and fuss with the little ones. It's more important for every tendril to be in place, and fewer flowers mean more gaps and awkward leanings. On the other hand, where large arrangements are imposing, smaller ones are often more charming. Filling wine glasses with cherry-tree blossoms and lining

them up on a table, or giving each guest an individual posy, is absolutely enchanting.

For a different, very contemporary look, but one that actually harks back to the old Dutch still lifes, consider vegetables, which make great centerpieces. Pick them for forms, colors, and durability—cauliflower and squash rather than tomatoes, which mold, and potatoes, which sprout eyes. Shape a damp dishcloth or towel into interesting contours inside a bowl or platter, on a cake stand, or in a cake basket, and then just arrange a selection of fruits and veggies on top. You can add dried flowers for textural variation. The current trend is for disparate combinations, but we've found that a good rule of thumb is to select flowers and vegetables in season.

Another traditional function of the pantry is to store linens—tablecloths, place mats, and napkins. If your linens are old or precious, it's best to store them in acid-free tissue. Even if your linens are relatively new, this is a good idea. Never use colored tissue. As well as being useful, napkins add a decora-

tive element to any table. If you have counter space, the pantry can be a good place to fold napkins—or to set up a young helper folding napkins into elaborate nineteenth-century shapes. Mrs. Beeton's guide is full of interesting and practical suggestions, which hosts and hostesses may enjoy practicing today.

OF ALL TABLEWARE, CHINA SEEMS TO EVOKE IN PEO-

PLE THE WIDEST EXTREMES OF FEELING. JOSEPH ADDI-

SON (1672–1719) REMARKED ON THE FONDNESS

THAT WOMEN, IN PARTICULAR, HAVE FOR PORCELAIN:

"THERE ARE NO INCLINATIONS IN WOMEN WHICH

MORE SURPRISE ME THAN THEIR PASSION FOR CHALK

AND CHINA. THE FIRST OF THESE MALADIES WEARS

OUT IN A LITTLE TIME, BUT WHEN A WOMAN IS VIS-

ITED BY THE SECOND, IT GENERALLY TAKES POSSES-

SION OF HER FOR LIFE." A CHARACTER IN EDITH

WHARTON'S *THE AGE OF INNOCENCE*, ON THE OTHER

HAND, IS THUS DISPARAGED: "WELL, I'LL TELL YOU

THE SORT: WHEN HE WASN'T WITH WOMEN HE WAS

COLLECTING CHINA. PAYING ANY PRICE FOR BOTH I

UNDERSTAND." SOME PEOPLE TREASURE SPECIAL

PLATES AND CUPS, WHILE THEY WOULDN'T DREAM OF

C H I N A

Previous pages and far right: These interesting pieces of Canton ware, most dating from 1700,

include a basketweave bowl and dish, a covered vegetable dish, a chocolate pot, a scallop-edged dish, sauceboats, and, opposite, a platter with a reticulated edge. Above: The teapot and teacup on the left are from Canton; the creamer, sugar bowl, additional cups, and muffin dish are from Nanking, another major manufacturing center.

using them; others are put off by the many confusing terms, glazes, and markings that distinguish fine china.

Porcelain and pottery can be intimidating. For true scholars and connoisseurs, it's an intriguingly complicated field, but to enjoy china at home, you need know only a few basic principles. Virtually every country has its own form of ceramics, from sun-baked pots to vessels fired in high heat, from coiled or thrown items to those fashioned in molds. The basic types of porcelain are hard and soft. Hard porcelain is a thin, white, durable, and often translucent material made of kaolin (a white clay with few impurities) and china stone, or petuntse, that is glazed, fired, and then glazed again. Soft porcelain is a combination of white clay and ground glass that is fired at a lower temperature than hard porcelain. Pottery differs from porcelain in that it is not vitrified or translucent; in addition, in most cases, without a glaze it would be porous. The two main types of pottery that are used for dishes are earthenware and stoneware.

The word *china* now covers all kinds of ceramic tableware, but at first it was used solely to describe porcelain ware imported from China. The Chinese perfected hard paste, as it's sometimes called, in the seventh and eighth centuries, but it wasn't until the fifteenth century that the first blue-and-white ware began to be imported to the West. Initially, this ware acted as ballast, stored in the deep holds of ships that carried exotic stores of tea, quicksilver, and silk; these lighter items could only travel in the upper, waterproof parts of the hull. But the Europeans admired the graceful new cups, saucers, bowls, and plates, far more delicate than their own heavy earthenware, and business was brisk. In England, for example, the first teapots were made of red-brown stoneware; wealthy families enjoyed the prestige of imported "China" or silver teapots, while those who couldn't afford the

more luxurious materials made do with pewter, faience, or Dutch delftware, the latter two being earthenware covered with a thick, opaque glaze.

A glassed-in china cabinet at Naumkeag stores a range of Chinese export ware dating from 1770 to 1795. In general, the smaller the teapot, the earlier it is, as tea was very expensive and leaves were savored. An exception to the rule, of course, are children's miniature porcelain tea sets, like the one on the top shelf.

Although Europeans manufactured a number of alternative ceramic forms, porcelain itself wasn't produced until 1709. Johann Friedrich Böttger, a young alchemist hired to make gold by Augustus the Strong of Saxony, discov-

ered instead how to make porcelain. A year later the famous factory at Meissen, near Dresden, was established, though it was several years before the formula was perfected. (Böttger is also credited with inventing a fine redware hard enough to be polished on a lapidary's wheel.) Espionage was rampant, and neighboring countries soon set up their own manufacturing firms; Austria, for example, became an important European porcelain-making center for rococo and Italianate tableware and figurines. In France, the Royal Porcelain Factory of Sèvres, founded in 1738 at Vincennes, produced exquisite hard porcelain and soft paste for the court of Louis XV. Madame de Pompadour, a great patron and taste setter, ordered bouquets made of hundreds of exquisitely colored porcelain flowers to fill her chambers. Today, early Sèvres and Meissen objects are worth a small fortune and are too fragile and important to use regularly, though both companies produced ware in the nineteenth century that might be appropriate for the grandest dinner. This doesn't mean you can't enjoy early objects—use them as decorative pieces on a table or mantelpiece.

This famille rose Chinese export teapot dates from the early 1700s.

These three plates are all examples of Oriental motifs as copied by English porcelain and ironstone makers between 1800 and 1840. Standard subjects such as temples, willow trees, pagodas, bridges, rocks, fretwork fences, fishing boats, jars, vases, and chrysanthemum blossoms were all interpreted in vivid colors according to Western notions of the East.

The French still have a tradition of exquisite porcelain; Sèvres continues to produce, as does Haviland & Co., founded in 1842 by a New York City retailer to produce French porcelain tableware for the American market. Haviland & Co. represented the pinnacle of fine china to many Americans, and supplied White House services to presidents Lincoln and Hayes.

Creamware, developed by Josiah Wedgwood, is a low-fired earthenware of a quality comparable to porcelain in fineness of body and lightness of color. This Staffordshire teapot dates from 1750.

The American and English appetite for Chinese export ware, characterized by bulbous or helmet-shaped pitchers, reticulated plates, leaf-shaped dishes, scalloped fruit bowls, globular teapots, and octagonal covered vegetable dishes, was enormous, lasting more than 150 years. The three major styles of Chinese export wares are known today as Nanking, Fitzhugh, and Canton. In 1765, George Washington received blue-and-white "Nankeen" mugs and a punch bowl with a "Nank" border, produced at Ch'ing-te-Chen, the great ceramics hub, then shipped down the Yangtze River from Nanking to the port of Canton, where it was sent to the West. Nanking ware is characterized by a central landscape with islands, rocks, trees, bridges, boats, and figures and a net-style border with objects in each mesh of the net; Canton ware offers somewhat cruder painting than Nanking, and is distinguished by the border—a dark blue lattice on a lighter blue ground with a scallop or wavy band. Fitzhugh, named for the East India Company's Canton representatives, features a circular medallion in the center, four floral panels, and a wide diaper (netlike), butterfly, or floral border. Sometimes Asian potters were commissioned to paint family crests and specialized European subjects, including landscapes, and the result can be a charming hybrid of styles.

*Like most manufactur-
ers, Meissen, the first
European company to
make porcelain (in 1710),
responded to the rage
for Oriental design
by creating its own
Eastern-inspired pat-
terns. "Pink Dragon"
dates from 1850.*

*This graphic, almost
geometric set was made
in 1770 by Dr. Wall, the
founding partner of
the Worcester porcelain
factory, which he man-
aged from 1751 to 1774.
The factory became
known as Royal
Worcester in 1862.*

All prominent nine-teenth-century families ordered china services that bore the family crest or monogram. Sèvres Royal Porcelain factory, founded in 1783, produced objects for Napoleon; this Second Empire plate was made for Napoleon III.

In addition to being used for candlesticks, gravy boats, leaf-shaped pickle dishes, and com-potes, creamware pro-vided exotic table garniture, like this pineapple-topped cen-terpiece with baskets holding porcelain strawberries. Following pages: An assortment of Stafford-shire and Yorkshire 1770–1790s creamware gleams in a display cab-inet, and, at right, typi-cal reticulated luncheon and dinner plates blend well with the pale colors of fruit.

The borrowing of culture went both ways. The great popularity of the Chinese, and, later, Japanese, style influenced European potters to imbue their ware with Oriental motifs. Like Meissen, which created a pink-dragon dinner service, virtually every manufacturer made popular patterns with distinctively Asian designs. One of the most famous blue-and-white patterns is in fact not Chinese at all but English. Depicting a sad story of two young lovers escaping a cruel and angry father, Willow became immediately popular. Josiah Spode first manufactured it in 1790, and then revised it, establishing the familiar scene of the weeping willow next to a bridge over which the ill-fated couple flees. Depending on which version you subscribe to, the birds flying overhead symbolize either the happy outcome of the story or serve as an ironic reference to the lovers' inability to escape. Incidentally, Willow is one of the longest-running patterns of all, which can making dating it problematic for novice collectors.

In England, the search for the formula for true porcelain resulted in various imitations, such as soft paste, which are today highly regarded in their own right. The first factory was established in 1745 at Chelsea; Bow and Derby followed, and then Worcester, founded by Dr. Wall. England's main manufacturing center, at Staffordshire, an area rich in clay beds and easily accessible by railroad, produced quantities of these wares, lead-glazed and decorated with enamels. Charming, whimsical, and beautifully crafted, these teapots and other objects are unfortunately extremely fragile, chipping and cracking easily, and are not able to withstand boiling water. In 1748, potters discovered that by adding bone ash to china clay and china stone they could make a material that was white, translucent, softer than hard paste, yet harder than soft paste. Less expensive to manufacture than porcelain, bone china, as it was called, became the standard English manufacturing medium during the nineteenth century.

While the English talent for making porcelain grew during the eighteenth century, the popular earthenwares that had been standard before the arrival of porcelain were still being manufactured. Creamware, a pale yellow or buff-colored earthenware, began replacing the popular delftware and tin-glazed faience on tables throughout England and America from about 1760. *Faience fine*, as creamware was called in France, was thin, lightweight, and less expensive to produce than porcelain. In 1765 the famous English potter Josiah Wedgwood presented his efforts to Queen Charlotte, wife of George III.

*At Naumkeag, a very
popular and charming
blue-and-white break-
fast service made by
Spode around the turn
of the century is
enhanced by the family's
glass and silver.
An early black-and-
white Staffordshire cof-
fee pot is printed in a
transferware pattern.*

She agreed to sponsor them, and the resulting "Queen's Ware" became highly successful. Much creamware is reticulated, with scalloped edges and lacy holes in the plate rims. The only drawback to creamware was that its color was not compatible with the favorite blue-and-white decorations of the day. So, fourteen years later, in 1779, Wedgwood introduced pearlware, which was similar to creamware except that the addition of white clay to the body and cobalt to the glaze made it much whiter, allowing the popular blue chinoiserie decoration to stand out. A lot of early pearlware is decorated with shell-edged rims painted blue.

Traditionally, decorations on ceramics are applied with glazes and hand painting. The object (sometimes first decorated with cobalt or manganese, a brownish purple) is glazed with feldspar and then fired at a very high temperature; afterward it is painted with enamel colors, which fuse to the glaze when fired at a low temperature. Very complicated, ornate pieces require many firings, as different colors and types of glazes and enamels fuse at different temperatures. In 1753, the invention of transfer printing—using "bats" or sheets of hardened gelatin and, later, paper tissues to apply patterns from engraved copper plates onto objects—revolutionized production, making it possible to issue fancy decorations on a grand scale. Transfer printing on pearlware marked the beginning of England's serious challenge to Chinese wares. Blue was the most common color, but by the 1820s pink, green, yellow, brown, black, and purple designs were also available. Flow blue, so called because of the "flow" powder added during firing that produced a desirable flowing together of the underglaze and transparent overglaze, was thought to re-create the haziness of earlier Chinese wares.

In 1805, Josiah Spode introduced stone china, a dense earthenware made with china stone, to compete more effectively with the multitude of imported Chinese porcelain wares. The grayish or blue hue of stone china was suitable for the ever-agreeable blue patterns. Ironstone, patented in 1813 by James Mason, was similar to stoneware, and both it and stone china were an improvement over pearlware, as they were hard, though nontranslucent, and could rival Chinese wares in whiteness and durability.

Stoneware, made in China even before porcelain, was first manufac-

tured in Europe in the Rhineland in the late 1500s. Beginning in the 1670s, the English matched these gray mugs, jugs, storage jars, chamber pots, and porringers decorated in cobalt blue with their own version in brown. Potters discovered that the addition of calcined flint produced a near-white high-fired body similar to porcelain. Stoneware (fired at a very high tem-

perature) does not require a glaze, as it's nonporous, but craftsmen realized that salt added during the firing process volatized to form a shiny, hard transparent glaze with an interesting texture, like that of an orange peel. Hundreds of "salt-glaze" wares were produced, and today are very desirable. The white varieties were molded into intricate shapes and patterns,

often decorated with the popular "scratch blue" incised designs of flowers, which were then filled with cobalt.

Potters also looked to Japan for inspiration, especially to Imari porcelains, which were very popular in England from 1820 to 1850 and typically had a basic design laid out in an underglaze blue; overglaze enamel colors, especially red and green, elaborated the pattern. In the 1880s and 1890s English potters produced numerous "Anglo-Japanese" patterns that featured cherry blossoms, birds, fans, and asymmetrical layouts. Sometimes gold or pink luster further embellished the wares. One of the unique patterns was Gaudy Welsh, made not in Wales but in Staffordshire. With a hand-painted polychrome floral decoration, Gaudy Welsh has great charm—it's very bright and almost primitive-looking—and, interestingly, was produced almost exclusively for German settlers in Maryland, Pennsylvania, and Delaware.

In 1795, Staffordshire boasted 150 separate factories; Josiah Wedgwood's experimentations made tea services widely available for the first time.

A collection of Stafford-shire transferware plates rests on a mantelpiece. Discovered in 1753, transfer printing made china decoration on a mass scale possible. Blue was the most common color, but by the 1820s a wide range of other colors were available, which are popular with collectors today.

Interest in early American history at the turn of the century encouraged china manufacturers to revive old historical designs. The series of N. Currier polychrome transferware dishes at left, made in England, depicts such scenes of American life and legend as "The Clippership Sweepstakes," "The Old Gristmill," and "American Homestead—Autumn." Also in vogue were religious sentiments, such as those in the Staffordshire plate above illustrating the peaceable kingdom.

Introduced by Minton at the 1851 Crystal Palace Exhibition, English majolica, like this sardine box with a fish-shaped handle, was often made to serve specific functions.

Covered cheese dishes, round or wedge shaped, make an attractive tableau for the dessert or supper table. Especially unusual is this 1862–1900 English stoneware dish modeled in the shape of a basket.

Wedgwood mixed different colored clays to produce wares that resembled marble, onyx, agate, and pebbles, in addition to his creamware. Other firms followed his lead, including Whieldon, whose name is still associated with these marbled objects. Minton, founded in 1793 and still active, is known for high-quality earthenware and bone china in numerous elegant patterns. In 1851, Minton introduced its version of Italian tin-glazed earthenware, majolica, which consisted of richly colored earthenware in naturalistic shapes—shells, pineapples, or leaves—often with other naturalistic forms like small fishes and reptiles added in full relief onto plates and inside cups. The more fanciful the better: oyster plates, nautilus-shell spoon warmers, and asparagus dishes were especially popular. Other important firms were, among others, Doulton, Cauldon, Coalport, Davenport, and Ridgway.

In America, despite the abundance of good raw materials, porcelain manufacturing never really developed, as there were few skilled craftsmen. In addition, until the 1850s, no tariff was imposed on imported goods to protect American products. However, in the 1870s, the ceramics industry organized itself to compete with Europe. Lenox, founded in 1889 as the Ceramic Art Company in Trenton, New Jersey, and still in business today, is probably America's most eminent manufacturer of bone china. But despite the successes, procelain wares were in general too expensive to produce. Instead, many American potters focused on less costly red, yellow, and white earthenwares, which were then decorated in innovative ways. Rockingham, with its yellowware body and mottled brown glaze, vaguely resembles tortoise shell; many finely modeled sculptural pitchers, teapots, plates, custard cups, and bottles were produced in Vermont, New Jersey, and Ohio. Spongeware, generally intended for kitchen use, had a yellowware or ironstone body that was decorated with a sponged-on cobalt-blue pattern. Redware platters, pans, dishes, and pie plates suited for everyday needs were decorated with trailed slip, or liquid clay, to create linear designs. The primary production centers were in New England, Pennsylvania, New York, Ohio, and the South.

This rare set of 1850s hand-painted oyster plates was produced at Sarreguemines, a French factory in the Lorraine region known for its naturalistic creations.

Whieldon ware, named for Thomas Whieldon (1719–1795), is an inventive, naturalistic, and highly collectible earthenware pottery whose marbled effect comes from mixing different clays and glazes.

The United States also has a strong tradition in art pottery. Dedham Pottery, which was founded in Chelsea, Massachusetts, and moved to Dedham in 1895, fashioned tableware with a crackle glaze, and, in a blue underglaze, featured borders painted with animals, flowers, and plant forms. The rabbit is the best-known design.

There are many ways to acquire china for the table, whether you wish to buy in bulk or merely supplement what you own or have inherited. Marks on porcelain, except on very early pieces, are generally straightforward. The larger companies usually marked the underside of their wares, either with initials or symbols, though these had a tendency to change over the years. Many ceramic wares in America bear the name of the company that imported them, rather than, or in addition to, the name of maker. Important china merchants included Shreve, Crump & Low; Ovington Bros.; Collamore & Co.; and Jones, McDuffee & Stratton. Size and style also relate to age—teapots that appear small enough to be a child's are often early examples dating from the period when tea leaves were exorbitantly expensive.

Far left: China patterns from the 1920s have a distinctive decorative style. They also mix well, as this grouping shows, with plates from Minton at bottom, and, at top from left to right, Wedgwood, Cauldon, and Wedgwood. Left: Services of this era also tend to be larger; this pattern, for example, has an eight-piece place setting—dinner, lunch, bread and butter plates, soup and sauce dishes, and a teacup and saucer—as compared to the five pieces offered by most manufacturers today.

In 1813, George and Charles Mason patented ironstone, a hard, white, non-translucent earthenware designed to compete with Chinese porcelain. Though much ironstone was left white after mid-century, boldly colored Japanese Imari-style decoration on ironstone and other earthenware was very popular throughout the 1800s.

One of the best ways to
mix and match china
patterns is to focus on a
color. Here, exuberant
Victorian roses accent
refined pink and gold
borders. The patterns
are a mix of Wedgwood,
Spode, Royal Chelsea,
and French porcelain
made for Tiffany & Co.

These timeless gold-
and-white classics cross
international lines. The
pieces here include items
from Limoges, Minton,
and Royal Bavarian.

These delicate hand-
painted dishes by vari-
ous Limoges
makers—Haviland, M.
Redon, and Porcelaine
Limousine—are typical
of French porcelain.

Spanning a century,
these Minton classics
mix delicate florals and
botanicals. Minton, one
of the major Stafford-
shire potteries, was
founded in 1793 and is
still in production today.

It's wise to remember a few things when handling ceramic objects. Always pick up any object with care, and even if a piece has a handle, support it from beneath—old teapots and

pitchers often have repaired spouts and handles, and ancient glue repairs are not always easy to see and may separate when least expected. In the past, many pieces of early pottery and porcelain have been repaired with metal staples, and sometimes finials, spouts, handles, and feet have been replaced with plaster. Metal staples,

which indicate an object was treasured enough to be repaired, won't necessarily diminish the value of old pieces and probably should be left alone. Skilled conservators, however, can generally replace or improve shoddy or discolored plaster repairs. Regularly check your items, and any you intend to buy, for hairline cracks. A minor nick on the rim probably won't matter, but even small fractures that extend from the rim into the body of a vessel could be a problem. You should avoid filling such objects with very hot or cold liquids.

Many ceramic objects, especially transfer-printed earthenware, pick up stains from years of exposure to gravy, tea, coffee, and other foods. It's possible to bleach these stains out, using chlorine bleach, hydrogen peroxide, and enzyme-based cleaners, but these methods require great care, especially on valuable objects—the bleaching agent can penetrate cracks in the glaze and ultimately lift the glaze (and design) off the body. By the way, early glazes were often made from lead, and dishes with such glazes should not be used for eating. Likewise, don't eat from a chipped or flaking dish.

China need not be a part only of the dining room. There are myriad ways to enjoy it throughout the house—dishes nestled on the bookcase or mixed among the objects on a *secrétaire*, flanking pictures on the wall or above door frames. Old odd saucers make good ashtrays or soap dishes, while a large platter in the hallway is an excellent receptacle for letters, gloves, and other accretions of daily life.

Dessert services, like
this one at far left from
E. V. Haugout & Co.,
gave license to luxury
and were some of the
fanciest china pro-
duced. At right, a cus-
tard stand, also called a
pot de creme set, has
cups for individual
servings.

NO DINING ROOM IS COMPLETE WITHOUT THE

SPARKLINGS OF GLASS, BE THEY FROM THE DELICATE

PRISMS OF A CHANDELIER OVERHEAD, THE INTRICATE

FACETS OF CANDLESTICKS ON THE MANTELPIECE, OR

A CLEAR BOWL FILLED WITH THE RICH DARK RED OF

CRANBERRY SAUCE OR THE SOFT GLOW OF RIPE

PEACHES. GLASS LOOKS BEAUTIFUL IN VIRTUALLY

EVERY GUISE: EITHER ALONE OR IN AN ARRANGEMENT

OF VESSELS OF DIFFERENT SIZES, SHAPES, AND COL-

ORS; EMPTY OR HOLDING BRIGHTLY COLORED

OBJECTS OR FOOD; POSITIONED TO CATCH THE

LIGHT OUTDOORS OR REFLECTING THE BRILLIANCE

OF SILVER ON A WELL-APPOINTED TABLE. WE TEND TO

ASSUME THAT GLASS IS GLASS, CLEAR AND FUNC-

TIONAL; IT IS, IN FACT, EXTRAORDINARILY VERSATILE,

RANGING IN THICKNESS FROM THE STURDINESS OF

OLD GREEN MADIERA BOTTLES TO GOSSAMER

THREADS MADE TO LOOK LIKE SPUN SNOW, AND, IN

G L A S S

decoration, from the nacreous finishes of ancient Rome, where glass was as prized as silver and gold, to the glittering textures and opaque, satiny surfaces of late-nineteenth-century crystal.

Though glass graced the tables of the elite in ancient Rome, it wasn't until the nineteenth century that glass became anything but a rich man's luxury, especially in America. Glass's traditional association, of course, is with the beverage service, as the primary function of glass has always been the storing and serving of liquids. The late eighteenth and nineteenth centuries saw some of the most elaborate, intricate, and inventive wine goblets ever produced: stems, called air twist, that appear to be twirling; whole scenes etched in frosted shadow or gardens splashed on with enamel; a rainbow of colors and a fountain of gold and gilding. Craftsmen experimented with all kinds of ornamentation—either by painting, enameling, or gilding an object or by cutting, engraving, carving, etching, or sandblasting designs, and sometimes using a combination of all these techniques. In their quest for ever-more-beautiful tablescapes, the Victorians recognized the importance

of glass, and pressed glass of the last century is an area in which America outstripped England (and most of Europe), both in terms of design and of technical excellence.

Essentially, glass is made of silica (sand), soda, and potash, components that fuse together in very hot temperatures and become crystalline as they cool. By altering the formula and adding metal oxides, glassmakers, who were often chemists by profession, dis-

covered they could change the color, clarity, and quality of glass. Lead crystal, out of which the finest cut glass is made, was developed in England by George Ravenscroft in 1675 and

Previous pages: An assortment of colored glass includes a pair of 1860 ruby flashed decanters, an 1875 Bohemian glass-and-silver claret jug, a ruby flashed biscuit barrel in the hobnail pattern, a mustard cup, and six 1850 punch cups on a silver-plated stand.

Glass lights up a room, whether found in chandeliers, candlesticks, or in table ornaments that reflect and refract light. Compare the everyday look of this room, at left, with its dressed-up counterpart, including rich jewel colors and vivid accent napkins, above.

resulted in a clearer, heavier, softer, and more brilliant glass than anything made before. Relatively little survives before the invention of lead, or "flint," glass, as earlier forms were much weaker and suffered numerous tiny cracks and fissures. The term *crystal* can cause confusion because it has become almost synonymous with the concept of fine glass. To glass scholars and curators, however, the word refers only to the mineral quartz or to a crystallized object. Now, to many dealers and buyers of glass, crystal denotes the highest, finest grade of glass available.

Of the three basic types of glass—free-blown, mold-blown, and pressed—free-blown glass is the earliest, though there's been a revival of the art among craftspeople today. The glassmaker attaches a lump of molten glass to a hollow rod, and then blows it, in the process turning and shaping it with various tools, including a long iron pontil. Often the bottom of a piece of free-blown glass bears a pontil mark, or "punty," a rough spot left by the pontil; the mark is not always readily discernible, however, as on later or finer pieces it has often been smoothed and polished out or ground off.

Previous pages: Glass shapes follow no hard and fast rules. This assortment dates from 1780 to 1890 and shows a range of decoration and styles. Air twist stems, also called ribbon stems, date from the mid-eighteenth century and are formed by trapping and twisting an air bubble into intricate spirals. Far left: Typical of the fanciful shapes of Venetian glass, this goblet has wing stems and applied flowers. Left: A series of ornate pink glassware made by Steuben in the 1920s and 1930s includes a cake bowl, goblet, cornucopia, and a pink-and-green candlestick.

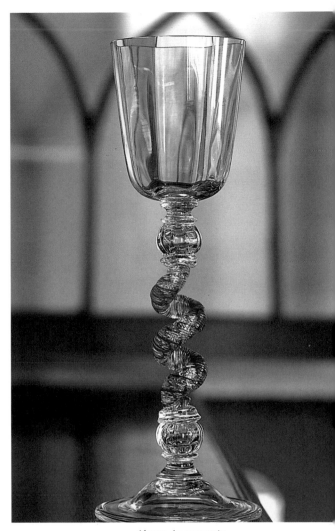

Above: An eccentric twist-stemmed goblet is laced with red. Left: Another wing-stemmed glass is swirled with opaque lines.

In 1739 in Salem, New Jersey, Caspar Wistar set up one of the earliest successful glass houses in America, producing mainly blown windowpanes, tumblers, and thick green bottles for that all-important commodity, whiskey. The average glass factory lasted only about ten years; the combination of wooden buildings and enormously hot furnaces resulted in many fires. In the 1760s, "Baron" Henry William Steigel of Manheim, Pennsylvania, experimented with dip, or part-size, molds that impressed patterns of ribs, diamonds, or panels onto bubbles of molten glass. As the bubble was blown to its full size, the pattern

expanded and softened, leaving surfaces that give the effect of sparkling light. The flamboyant Steigel proclaimed his wares equal to any imported from abroad, and indeed it's virtually impossible to distinguish his from pieces of the same period fabricated in Europe. Pattern-molded Steigel bottles, often executed in blue or amethyst, are rare and highly desirable today.

The invention of mold-blown glass, produced from 1815 to 1845 by such companies as the New England Glass Co., Boston & Sandwich, and Gillander Glass Co., made large quantities of table glass available for the first time. For mold-blown glass, the molten bubble is blown into a full-size mold that forms and decorates the object simultaneously. These molds, made for decanters, wineglasses, tumblers, caster bottles, tea or dessert plates, celery vases, creamers, sugar bowls, and cruets, come in two, three, or four pieces (three is the most common, and glass made in such a mold is referred to as "blown-three-mold" glass); characteristic of the style are the seams that run the length of the object where parts of the mold hinged. Though the form was originally meant to imitate English and Irish cut glass, and rims, lips, feet, and handles were finished by hand, the surfaces are more rounded, the patterns less crisp, and the lines softer than those of cut glass. Collectors divide mold-blown glass into three styles, geometric, baroque, and Gothic, after the propensities of the patterns.

Then, in 1828, Deming Jarves of the Boston & Sandwich Glass Company patented an "improvement" that mechanically pressed molten glass into molds, the first major innovation in glass-making techniques in more than two thousand years. The invention of pressed glass, smooth on the interior and patterned on the exterior, made production on a grand scale possible

Although there was plenty of variety previously, it wasn't until the late nineteenth century that glass shape denoted content. This exquisite set, made by the French company Val St. Lambert, shows an elaborate place setting. The tall glasses, in descending order of height, are for water, red wine, and sherry. The rounder glasses are for white wine and champagne. A finger bowl and its dish complete the service. A cameo cut-glass Val St. Lambert decanter sports heavy gold banding.

Drawing on the popularity of Bohemian glass, many American manufacturers produced wares stained or flashed with ruby. George Duncan & Sons made this beaded-dart glassware with flashed ruby bands in 1880. The pitcher is red-flashed King's Crown, also called Giant Thumbprint, and was produced by Adams & Co. in the 1880s.

Some historians argue that, in an era of abstinence, cut and pressed glass like this 1890s heavy cut-glass water pitcher, was so desirable because it looked as pretty holding water as it looked holding wine.

Right: This English mahogany chest and cut-glass decanter set dates from 1820. The silver decanter labels, an elegant innovation developed during the days when glass bottles were so murky their contents couldn't be seen, date from 1850. The small glasses with the white-and-gold enamel design are from Bristol, an English glass-making center.

One of the most beautiful and sought-after early pressed-glass types today is Lacy glass, whose stippled surface (disguising any imperfections) and intricate patterning give the appearance of lace. Salt cellars, saucers, bowls, tea and cake plates, compotes, trays, sugar bowls and creamers, sauce boats, candlesticks, covered entree dishes, and butter dishes were most often colorless, but some were produced in shades of amethyst, blue, yellow, and green, as well as opalescent blue and white and opaque white opal, or milk, glass. Milk glass is an interesting field on its own: only a few hundred patterns were made, as opposed to the thousands in clear or colored pressed glass, and complete sets are rare; look instead for individual pitchers, sugar bowls, compotes, or, most desirable of all, covered dishes with animals—hens, rabbits, ducks—resting on top.

The latter half of the nineteenth century saw the rise of patterned glass on an unprecedented scale. As in other areas, it's hard to say whether demand created the technology or technical innovation caused the demand; what's clear is that, along with silver and china, glass became another way for prosperous middle- and upper-middle-class diners to show off. Because so much was made, it is still possible to find complete sets today. Early patterns paralleled the preference for Grecian and classical designs in buildings and furnishings, with motifs of flutes, panels, honeycombs, diamonds, and reeding. These are the most valued today; in particular, look for Flute, Excelsior, Argus, Ashburton, Colonial, Honeycomb, Diamond Thumbprint, and Bellflower, patterns that were frequently made by more than one manufacturer, although they might have different names.

In 1864, a West Virginia glassmaker discovered a formula for glass that dramatically changed production. Cheaper and quicker to make, the new soda-lime glass was also lighter and less expensive to ship. The lower cost of production enabled glassmakers to divert funds to design, and to experiment more heavily with color. Some connoisseurs feel the results lack the refractive brilliance and weight of earlier forms made with lead, but others see the period as innovative and exciting, filled with both excellent and inferior examples. Patterns became more naturalistic, weaving together flower and vine motifs, animals, human figures, and heads. In the 1870s, frosting and acid etching, both on clear and colored glass, became fashionable. Designs include Three Faces (patented by George Duncan & Sons, Pittsburgh), with three classical frosted heads forming the finials, or handles, on covers, the stems of glasses and compotes, and the bodies of salt shakers; Lion, with lion finials, and Actress (introduced about 1885 by LaBelle Glass Company, Bridgeport, Ohio), with portraits of popular theater stars.

Previous pages: A frosted glass goblet in the Tree of Life pattern, embellished with a gold rim and an applied red snake twining up the stem, was made by the Boston & Sandwich Glass Co. in the 1860s. A collection of 1920s–1930s gold-banded cut-glass stemware and a tankard wine pitcher are on display at Blantyre.

Glassware from the collection at Naumkeag includes, from left, a fitted sherbet coupette with dish, a red wine glass with color overlay, two sizes of a series of colored mold-blown glasses, and a white-wine glass with a diamond-cut band and color inlay. Swirled ribbon glass like that shown here was made in Venice and Nailsea, a glassmaking center in England. Above: The silver frame on this set of Continental pressed-glass acid-etched salt cellars made storage easy.

The development of
pressed glass in 1828
started a century-long
period of exploration
with a variety of forms
for serving and drinking.
Even among clear glass,
the range is enormous.
Above, an unusually del-
icate acid-etched depres-
sion glass pattern, called
Diana, was made by the
Cambridge Glass Co. in
the 1930s. At right, a
slightly grayish tint gives
this diamond-cut pattern
a very modern feel. The
glasses are for, from left,
water, white wine, red
wine, cordials, and
champagne.

The difference between cut and pressed glass can be seen in the crispness of the design on the outside. On the inside, cut glass tends to be smoother, while pressed glass often has an embossed feeling. This group of pressed glass dates from 1850–1880.

The glass on its side at the left is called Horn of Plenty, made by Bryce McKee in the 1850s. Behind it is Honeycomb with Diamond, made by Blakewell, Pears & Co. in 1864. The big glass is called Open Rose, made by the Boston & Sandwich Glass Co. in the 1870s. At far right is Pineapple, made by the New England Glass Co. in 1860.

In the last two decades of the nineteenth century, geometric patterns, in particular the widely popular Daisy and Button design, were often flashed and/or stained with gilt or translucent colors, to imitate earlier Bohemian glass. By the turn of the century, the rise of the Colonial Revival style inspired simpler patterns, with fluted, block, or thumbprint motifs. Depression glass, made during the 1920s and 1930s, features delicate pressed or acid-etched neoclassical patterns in pale green, pink, blue, or amber. Unlike earlier sets, the primary function of which was to display and serve food, depression glass offered all the individual pieces, including coffee cups and saucers, necessary for eating.

Even though most families ate their meals on ceramic dishes, they still ordered quantities of glassware to complement the setting. A typical pattern, like the New England Glass Company's New York, included thirty-six separate items: ale glass, beer mug, bowls, candlesticks, Champagne glass, claret glass, cordial glasses, custard glass, decanter, egg glass, finger bowl, goblet, ketchup bottle, lemonade glass, molasses jug, nappy (a small dish with two handles), pickle jar, spoon glass, sugar and creamer, and wineglass. In 1873, the domestic adviser Elizabeth Ellet recommended that housewives have on hand "three dozen wine glasses, two dozen champagnes, two dozen claret glasses, three dozen goblets, six water carafes, six decanters, one liqueur stand, twelve liqueur glasses, two glass pitchers, one celery stand, one trifle bowl, and eight dessert dishes." In addition, some specialty lines made available ice-cream trays with matching saucer and ice canoe (a boat-shaped glass bowl), covered cake plates, match safes for storing matches, celery yacht and corresponding salt yacht (containers for these items shaped like boats), sugar casters, oil cruets, and hurricane-lamp or gasolier shades to match the table glass. Glass and silver were paired together to make all manner of objects for drinking and serving: decanters and stands, revolving caster sets, and pickle jars with silver mounts.

Though many of these items are still useful in their original functions, some we might wish to adapt to modern life. Bread plates now make good dinner plates, while six-inch glass tea plates are still appropriate for cake and dessert. Spooners and celery vases are handy for flowers, while sugar bowls suit as candy jars, and several stacked cake stands, filled with flowers or fruit, make pretty centerpieces. Wedding gifts from the late 1800s, such as violet glass dishes trimmed with silver, green glass bowls with gold decoration, or lavender rose bowls with gold ornamentation, are just as beautiful today as they were a century ago.

In addition to the popularity of pressed and patterned glass, the Victorian love of ornamentation found expression in luxury, or art, glass—that is, glass made primarily for display. Usually richly colored, these vases, bowls, epergnes, wine jugs, finger bowls, and goblets were also ornately decorated, either enameled, engraved, embellished with applied glass threading or gilding, or combined with silver. The tradition of colored glass in the United States can be traced to Bohemia, a major glassmaking center since the sixteenth century. Known particularly for the ruby-colored varieties, Bohemian glass, and American glass made in the Bohemian style, is often engraved with grapes and vines or hunt scenes, and used espe-

Silver and glass are natural partners. At left, a small everyday cruet stand holds oil, vinegar, pepper, and mustard, served with a spoon. For serious spicing, there's the elaborate 1890 Victorian rococo silver-plated condiment stand at right; two of the eight bottles have sterling silver lids. Below: In an age that pickled everything, pickle jars were a necessity. This elegant 1870s American pressed-glass pickle caster in the Star and Block pattern has small forks and silver-plated scrolling.

Following pages: Covered dishes made an attractive and sanitary way to serve butter. Shown here are a variety of pressed-glass examples from 1850–1880, including the perennial favorite, a recumbent cow. (In the back is a lone Frosted Ribbon cheese dish.) At right, pressed-glass sweetmeat dishes and open and covered sugar bowls make good candy or nut servers.

cially for decanters, wineglasses, and pitchers. The great exhibition in 1851 at the newly built Crystal Palace in London introduced consumers to other European glass forms, and American manufacturers strove to produce more and more elaborate pieces, in all shapes, with every conceivable decoration. Technical innovations characterized the period. One popular style was cased glass, in which objects were made from several different colored bands layered from the inside of the object outward. Glassmakers created multicolored designs by cutting through from one layer to another. Also called overlay, this form is often seen in white and ruby, green, or blue, with the outer layers carved through to show the pattern on the innermost layer. Cameo glass is cased glass in which the outer layer carries the design.

In enameling, decorations are painted onto the surface of the glass and then fired in a kiln. The Smith Brothers, the Mount Washington Glass Company, and the Boston & Sandwich Glass Company were the most important American producers of enameled glass, generating wares embellished with flowers, landscapes, and exotic motifs, often in conjunction with silver.

Other methods for applying color were staining, plating, lining, and flashing. As ruby was one of the favorite colors of the fin de siècle, clear patterned glass was often brushed with a ruby stain to add a touch of elegance. This period was also called the Gilded Age, and one manifestation was the gilt used liberally on glass edges and in patterns; a bride received a dozen tumblers, goblets, dessert dishes, finger bowls, and plates, all trimmed with a gold border. Color experimentation led to special heat-treated wares like Amberina, each piece of which is shaded from amber to ruby; opaque Peachblow, containing graduated colors from white to pale pink; and Burmese, which ranges from yellow to soft rose on each piece. (Queen Victoria ordered two pairs of Oriental-looking Burmese-glass vases.) Satin Glass, originally called Pearl Satin, had a lusterless "soft finish" surface achieved by sandblasting that was often supplemented with enameling. Most distinctive was its quilted appearance, resulting from trapped air bubbles, and its ruffled rim. A variation, called Coralene, fused glass beads over an enameled coral-like decoration.

Cut glass, which had been in fashion at the beginning of the nineteenth century, became more accessible as nineteenth-century wealth increased, and from the 1880s until the 1920s, "brilliant cut," as it was called, was the most desirable and expensive type of glass. Where a caster set in Amberina cost $8.50, for example, or $11.00 in Burmese, a cut-glass version would set you back $16.75. Cut glass is glass in which the pattern is actually ground away, not cut, by wheels that make the decoration. The discovery of loads of relatively iron-free sand in the Midwest led to finer, clearer cut glass. The Libby Glass Co., Heisey Glass, and Steuben and T. G. Hawkes & Co. in Corning were some of the companies that specialized in cut glass. The multifaceted surfaces of berry bowls and ice-cream sets created a glittering display on dinner-party tables. Punch-bowl sets were extremely prestigious, and brilliant-cut place settings included goblets, red wine, white wine (sometimes cased with colored glass), Champagne, sherry, and cordial glasses, plus a finger bowl and an underplate. Many glass manufacturers, such as Pairpont, shipped heavy lead-glass "blanks" to be cut by smaller companies that specialized in fine finishing. In fact, some unscrupulous glassmakers went over

pressed-glass patterns with a cutting wheel to further heighten the piece's brilliance; these pieces can be deceptive, but check the inside of the bowl—glass cut from blown blanks is generally smooth, while pressed pieces often have an embossed feeling. The labor-intensive process of cutting glass was a valued one in the era of the arts-and-crafts movement and the renewed interest in artisan traditions and craftsmanship by hand. The first brilliant-cut glass pattern, Russian, patented in 1882 by T. G. Hawkes & Co., was so widely admired that President Benjamin Harrison ordered a set for the White House in 1886. Other popular patterns include Strawberry Diamond and Fan, Hobnail, and Honeycomb.

Glass is inherently fragile and must be handled with care. Be especially careful of handles—when carrying a pitcher or jug, provide extra support from beneath the piece. The rim is the most vulnerable part of most glasses and will chip easily. Some chips can be ground or polished away, but not all, and not always without some noticeable loss of material. When you put glasses away in the cupboard, be sure that outward-flaring rims don't bump each

This assortment of milk jugs and creamers in flint and non-flint glass includes the patterns Cut Log, Diamond Thumb-print, Northwoods Cherry, and Dart. Right: Glass compotes still look best as receptacles for fruit. Richards & Hartley made this pattern, Cupid and Venus, in 1875.

other. Remember that, with some early American glass, frosting, engraving, or enameling may have been used to disguise inherent weaknesses in the quality of the glass. Also, both blown glass and cut glass tend to be weaker than pressed glass because of alternating thick and thin areas.

Glass is subject to thermal shock, so avoid sudden temperature changes when washing and storing. Never put a pitcher that has recently contained cold liquid—water, iced tea, lemonade—into hot water. Wait until the glass has come to room temperature, and use lukewarm water to wash. And remember that glass is slippery, especially when wet. When you move glass from a very cold place to a warmer spot, allow it to remain in its packing materials until it reaches room temperature. Any sudden change may cause glass to shatter or crack. Some glasses can be replaced through a pattern-matching service, but not always. Getting white lime deposits out of decanters can be tricky—try a commercial water softener. Soapy ammonia and bottle brushes help with wine sediment

As few factories marked their pieces, and popular patterns, under different names, were produced by more than one factory, it can be difficult to date and identify pieces today. Furthermore, craftsmen tended to move from company to company, which makes attributing hard. The important factors in determining age are weight, color, and clarity of pattern. (Dealers and curators have access to lights that detect sand content and defects for both pressed and flint glass.) Also keep in mind stylistic changes as possible dating indicators. Here are some general guidelines: in the second half of the nineteenth century, glasses became more slender, with longer stems; Regency-period decanters have high shoulders and rounded stoppers, while later examples often have gently sloping sides and oval stoppers. And, when buying, check lids, covers, and stoppers both for chips or cracks and for period compatibility.

As in any field, "designer brands," pieces attributed to particular craftsmen or factories, have cachet. But be wary of buying imitations. Mary Alice Gregory, for example, was a young painter hired by Boston & Sandwich in 1880 to decorate glasswares; but today she is associated mostly with certain enameled figures in the Kate Greenaway style, which are considered highly desirable. Even shops in Europe purport to carry her work. But no fragments have been found at Sandwich, which has led some scholars to believe that an unscrupulous Sandwich antiques dealer started the Mary Gregory legend in 1921 in the hopes of improving business. Most dealers will stand behind their wares, but it's always a good idea for the buyer to be as informed as possible. The one rule of thumb is this: if you are buying something because you love it, you can't go wrong.

IN CERTAIN CONTEMPORARY CIRCLES, SILVER HAS

BEEN OUT OF FASHION—SO STUFFY, SOME PEOPLE

SAY, TOO MUCH TROUBLE TO CLEAN, TOO HARD TO

STORE. BUT OTHERS KNOW BETTER. "SILVER," AN

OLD FRIEND OF MINE ONCE REMARKED, "IS A

ROOM'S JEWELRY." EVEN IF WE DON'T USE OUR

SILVER BOWLS AND MUFFINEERS IN THE WAY THE

S I L V E R

MAKERS INTENDED, BUT INSTEAD KEEP THEM ON

THE MANTELPIECE, THEY IMPART A TOUCH OF ELE-

GANCE. SILVER ADDS A SPARKLE TO EVERY OCCA-

SION, DRESSES UP EVERY EVENT, AND MAKES EVEN A

FAMILY MEAL SPECIAL. SO BEFORE RELEGATING

THOSE ENORMOUS SERVING BOWLS TO THE VAULT

OR FOREGOING THE PURCHASE OF A MARROW

SPOON BECAUSE IT'S NOT USEFUL, CONSIDER HOW

TO INCORPORATE THESE TREASURES INTO DAILY LIV-

ING. AT FIRST GLANCE, SILVER SEEMS LIKE AN INTIMI-

dating field. There's the value to consider, the markings, the technical terms. In fact, a little knowledge goes a long way with silver, particularly English silver, because its history is so well documented. This, in addition to the fact that a lot was made and, because it's not easy to break, a lot has survived, means there's less chance for fraud than in other areas. The first thing to understand is that pure silver is too soft for items meant to be used every day and has traditionally been alloyed with copper, which acts as a strengthening agent. Sterling silver, a standard set in England in the twelfth century and adopted in America in 1868, describes fineness, or percentage of pure silver, and translates as .925 parts silver to .075 parts copper. During the second quarter of the nineteenth century, American silver was often marked coin, coin silver, dollar, or standard, all of which refer to the fineness of coins in circulation at the time (from 1792 to 1837, .8924; from 1837 onward, .900).

Silver plate joins a thin coating of silver to another metal, and is therefore less expensive than sterling silver. The first kind of silver plate was Sheffield

Previous pages: Gorham's Chantilly pattern has been available continuously since 1895. Some of the more than 100 different shapes include (clockwise from top right): a cheese knife, a lemon fork, sugar tongs, butter knife, baby-food pusher, oyster fork, a salad fork, tea bell, a fruit fork, another butter knife, an ice-cream fork, a napkin marker, fruit knife, and a strawberry fork resting over a two-pronged olive fork. In the center are a cheese spreader and a three-pronged olive fork. Above: Once fairly standard for upper-middle-class homes, boxed silver sets, or canteens, like this English seven-piece service for twelve with room for serving pieces underneath, are greatly prized today.

plate, which was made by fusing thin strips of silver around a thicker band of copper. Accidentally discovered in the 1740s, it quickly caught on, as it offered the latest fashions at more affordable rates than sterling. In the mid-nineteenth century, a new technology called electroplating, which transferred silver atoms via electric currents to pewter or white metal objects, revolutionized the silver industry. Though Sheffield plate is still made, Old Sheffield plate (pre-1838) is highly valued today, not as silver's poorer cousin, but in its own right.

Hallmarks appear on every silver object made in England since 1327. This series of signs includes the maker's mark (name, initials, or symbol); a date in the form of a letter; a town mark (a leopard's head indicates London); a fineness mark (a lion passant means sterling); and a duty mark of a king or queen's head, though this was discontinued in 1890. Identifying American silver is a bit trickier, since no formalized system was ever adopted. Some companies used date marks, while others stamped on pseudo-hallmarks. Always check the marks, though—partnerships were formed and dissolved

Some grand old Berkshires houses are fitted with vaults for storing the family silver. The ordinary collector might want to fix up a closet with a good lock and lined shelves.

so quickly that it's usually possible to date a piece within a few years. Tiffany & Co. began using "English sterling" in 1854, and, after 1868, silver manufacturers simply said "sterling." Electroplated pieces may read "EPNS," which means electroplated nickel silver. (The two main alloys used in electroplating are nickel silver and Britannia metal, both white metals.) Other stamps are "triple plate" and "quadruple plate," terms used by manufacturers to indicate higher-quality wares, with a thicker layer of plating.

When people talk about silver today, more often than not they mean flatware. A set of silver flatware is a bride's dream, whether an heirloom handed down through the family or bought spanking new. In the history of silver, flatware is a relatively recent development. Early flatware is limited almost exclusively to spoons, ladles, tongs, and barbaric-looking two-pronged forks; elegant forks, knives, and spoons were made in the seventeenth and eighteenth centuries, but these were

owned only by royalty and very wealthy families. It wasn't until the nineteenth century that new technical developments—electroplating, steam-powered drop presses that stamped out enormous quantities of specialized shapes, and engine turning, a technique for decorating hollowware—made the mass production of silver patterns possible. In 1869, three times as much electroplate was being produced as sterling, and selling for a quarter the cost.

To dine elegantly at the table in the early nineteenth century required a tablespoon for soup, an ivory-handled fish knife and fork, a dinner knife and fork, and a dessert fork and spoon, all in a relatively simple pattern. A soup ladle, gravy spoons, and possibly asparagus tongs would take care of the serving. Few people had silver in a complete pattern; until the late nineteenth century, knives, with handles of pearl, ivory, bone, or ebony, usually formed their own set, as did the fish service and the dessert service.

In the Victorian age, dining was an extremely serious business and flatware makers prospered as a result, offering designs as diversified and particular as possible. Objects of once homely utility were elevated to the status of art. Mass production symbolized progress, and owning a vast quantity of the new electroplated objects was a sign of status. As technology facilitated the transition from handmade to machine made, manufacturers began producing more elaborate patterns in greater variety.

A Victorian breakfast-time favorite, eggs received enormous attention from craftsmen, who developed elaborate tablewares, often based on earlier designs, to better serve them. Far left: An 1880 egg basket, when filled with boiling water, made it possible to finish cooking eggs right at the table. Left: A silver-plated egg coddler kept the egg warm at table. This page: A medley of toast and egg racks ranging from 1860 to 1910 are displayed on a tiered table. Note particularly the 1869 silver plate "Donkey Cart" egg and toast server, the eggshell-shaped cup, and egg and toast stand with spoons and room for marmalade.

The expression "below the salt" refers to the days when salt was a valuable commodity, slated only for the nobler folk, who sat "above" the salt cellar at a long table. Since the 1750s, cobalt glass has traditionally lined silver salt cellars, including sentimental figural favorites like "Boy on a Fence." An arrangement of cake baskets complements the still life in Edith Wharton's dining room. This group of baskets, produced between 1840 and 1920 by Meriden & Co., James Dixon & Son, and William Hutton & Son, look marvelous when filled with cookies, fruit, or flowers.

Gorham introduced two new patterns in the 1840s, three more in the 1850s, and seventeen in the 1860s; many are modifications of traditional themes, but others are more eccentric: Bird's Nest has a little silver nest and egg at the tip of each piece, while Medallion features a series of different classical heads on the key utensils.

By the 1880s, the table furniture for an ordinary society dinner had become three times greater than its 1840s counterpart. With meals that often encompassed eight courses (and,

Far left: The woman who gathered these teaspoons began collecting as a little girl. Inexpensive and easy to find, each one is different, and, though kept in a pressed-glass spooner, most are used daily. In the background is her grandmother's Meriden Co. sugar bowl.

Below left: Historically an exotic luxury, sugar has always been given lavish treatment at the table. Late 1800s Dutch, English, and American sugar holders range from wide-mouthed scuttles with a scoop attached to a trough for cubes to bowls equipped with teaspoons.

Right: The advent of granulated sugar prompted the making of shakers, casters, or sifters resembling earlier muffineers. This group dates from the turn of the century.

Left: Mustard has been a favorite condiment at least since the fifteenth century. This pierced silver mustard pot dates from the mid-nineteenth century.

on special occasions, upwards of fifteen), at the very least a place setting would contain two large knives, three large forks (for game, roast, and entrees), a fish knife and fork, one or two soup spoons (for clear and cream soups), and an oyster fork. Salad forks, dessert forks and spoons, and any additional utensils (strawberry forks, for instance, or orange spoons) for the dessert course were brought in at the appropriate moment.

Boxed gift sets were immensely popular for weddings, Christmas, and anniversaries, and were intended to supplement existing silver services. Nestled in a silk-, satin-, or plush-lined leather box, they are still extremely useful and cover every eating contingency from fish to ice cream. Look for berry sets (a berry spoon and six forks); pastry or pie sets; chocolate sets (a muddler and six chocolate spoons); salad sets with servers and forks; coffee sets (demitasse spoons, small sugar tongs, and sometimes a cream ladle); tea sets; oyster, butter, and nut sets; fruit sets with six fruit knives; a dessert set (including a cake knife, an ice-cream knife, a berry spoon, a pie knife, and a waffle knife); and carving sets.

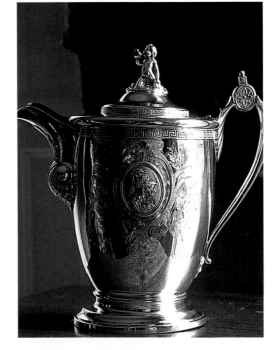

Far left: The nineteenth century was a time of innovation and constant technical advancement, with manufacturers vying to create newer, more elaborate serving dishes, like this silver-plated 1865 revolving tureen whose lid pops open. Left: A grand 1873 Reed & Barton soup tureen might have ushered in the first course. Below: A classically inspired 1880 silver plate water pitcher, also made by Reed & Barton, has a ceramic liner to keep water cold longer, a design patented in 1868.

The last quarter of the nineteenth century was the golden age of American silver flatware production—Gorham alone produced fifty-five patterns in one decade. Enormous complete sets were the vogue, ensconced in their own wooden chests. (Today, a complete set in its case is worth far more than the same set collected piecemeal.) A well-to-do bride might receive from her industrialist papa a set of Meriden Britannia for twelve, including: dinner and dessert knives; dinner and dessert forks; table, dessert, tea, and coffee spoons; a soup ladle, berry spoon, sugar shell, sugar tongs, butter knife, ice tongs, salad spoon and fork, pie knife, fish knife, fork, and carver. Also available were spoons for olives, eggs, and ice cream, mustard, salt, nuts, macaroni, and gravy; forks for pickles and oysters; knives for fruit and ice cream; tongs for salad, asparagus (individual and serving), and sardines; ladles for soup, punch, gravy, cream or sauce, and fruit; a cheese

scoop, a julep strainer, a jelly shell, a preserve shell, a cake cutter, a crumb knife, nut picks, nut cracks, and grape shears. Though of the same pattern, all of these would be different from one another in size, with variation in the shape of the spoons' bowls, the forks' tines, and the degree of ornamentation.

To Victorian craftsmen, purity of design was irrelevant, and to a hodgepodge of historical styles they joined a strong influence from Japan, the sinuous lines of naturalism, and the English

Silver styles vary enormously. Compare the grand embellishments of this nineteenth-century Tiffany water urn—inspired by a seventeenth-century design—with the sleek lines of this art nouveau coffee service.

aesthetic and arts-and-crafts movements. In an age awed by the possibilities of the machine, the more ornate, intricate, and specialized the better. Victorian craftsmen experimented with all the traditional forms of decoration and invented others, which could be executed by hand or by machine: gilding the bowls of spoons and the interiors of cream pitchers (the gold was thought to taste better with certain delicate or acidic foods);

engraving, or peeling thin filaments off an object's surface with a diamond-shaped steel rod called a graver; chasing, or indenting, metal in a linear pattern; and embossing, punching the metal from the back to create raised beading (a line of round "bosses") on the front. In acid etching, a surface was covered with wax except where the design was to appear. Repoussé combined chasing and embossing to create a design in high relief on the front of the object. First the design was chased on the outside, then the chased areas were hammered out into lumps of desired size and shape from the inside with a snarling iron. Gadrooning, a variation of repoussé, meant a decorative raised border, frequently seen on candlesticks or the rim of a vase. Fluting was the reverse, grooved in instead of out.

In addition to flatware, three-dimensional serving items (called hollowware) proliferated as the aesthetic of the industrial age prevailed.

The size of place set-
tings has alternately
grown and shrunk in the
last 200 years. The
important thing to
remember is that, in
general, the number of
utensils corresponds to
the number of courses.
Above, on either side of
Coalport's 1810–1840
Bow pattern, French
vermeil flatware is laid
face down to display the
crest, or, in this case,
engraving (a holdover,
too, from the days when
guests might catch their
lace cuffs on upturned
prongs).

An early-nineteenth-century family meal might have used hand-made pistol-handled knives and three-tined forks like these above, while a mid-nineteenth-century table setting, like that at right, might have mixed a special ivory-handled fish service with other flatware.

This round-up of highly ornamented glass-and-silver biscuit barrels and boxes dates from between 1865 and 1875. Note the lamb atop one and the dog atop another, and the unusual folding muffin warmer at left, made by Elkington.

Pewter, an alloy of tin and lead, lends an early American flavor to salt cellars, tankards, and teapots. Of particular interest is an unusual early pepper mill with ivory feet and, at bottom, an 1850 English silver marrow spoon.

If anything could be made to move, swivel, or spring, it was. Covered dishes stood like armies along the sideboard keeping their contents warm; when needed, their lids sprang back to reveal glistening peas, mounds of onions in cream sauce, or prawns in custard. Sparkling waters were a fashionable alternative to wines and spirits, and tilting water pitchers were made with a double lining of either silver or porcelain to keep the contents cool longer. Many objects were designed thematically: Champagne buckets decorated with polar bears and glaciers, citrus presses fashioned to look like enormous overwrought lemons, wine coolers covered with cascading grape leaves. Other hollowware included napkin rings, centerpieces and epergnes, menu holders, placecard holders, knife rests, toothpick holders, and service bells.

The Victorian love of fancy found expression even in the smallest objects that were made for serving condiments. Apart from sugar bowls, shakers, and tongs, sugar cubes were served in troughs and wide-mouthed scuttles, complete with a scoop at the back, which paid homage to the thriving mining industry of the day. Today, many collectors of sugar implements have them on hand to serve different kinds of sugar: lump, powdered, rock, brown, packaged, and, of course, pure granular. In addition, as collecting souvenir spoons became an essential part of tourism, manufacturers turned out spoon racks by the hundreds. Some came as part of tea sets, connected to the sugar bowl, while others were sold individually. The 1890s also saw a revival of the eighteenth-century Georgian spoon tray. And salt cellars, often lined with cobalt glass to prevent salt from corroding the silver, were shaped into every imaginable form: beautiful seashells, exotic boats, domestic scenes.

Many of these very specialized accessories are useful today. Delicate, pierced cake baskets, when not used for their original purpose, act as beautiful, decorative

During the last quarter of the nineteenth century, silver salt cellars and other objects took on exotic or romantic motifs, like Cupid perched on a boat, above, or this large naturalistic salt dish, above right. At far right is a patriotic American sterling silver salt dish with an eagle made by Whiting in 1880. Dominick and Hoff fashioned the heart-shaped dish at right in 1890.

containers for flowers, fruit, or an unusual arrangement of legumes; they also serve as a gracious way to hold napkins at a buffet. Biscuit barrels and muffin baskets—cut, pressed, or patterned glass capped with silver—make wonderful ice buckets. Toast racks are handy for letters or napkins, while some ornate candlesticks perform superbly as floral stands.

If you're thinking about buying silver, there are several things to keep in mind. Nineteenth-century flatware is often a much better buy than its contemporary equivalent, plus it will have the patina of time and age. A well-established name like Tiffany & Co., Gorham, Rogers Brothers, Kirk, or Reed & Barton gives a piece cachet (and will usually be more expensive), but there are plenty of lesser-known companies that produced fine wares. Certain patterns are more valued than others, either because they're famous (like Gorham's Chantilly or Tiffany's Chrysanthemum), rare because, like Lap Over Edge, they include a lot of hand finishing. Make sure that the raised design is crisp and that any monograms are original to the piece and not rubbed out or added years later.

Silver plate is difficult to repair, as the heat from soldering can melt the Britannia metal body. Dents, though, can be hammered out carefully, and skilled silver restorers can recast lost parts. (Check with a local museum for reputable restorers.) Don't replate unless you really have to—replating can be done, but it may diminish the value of fine pieces, as it tends to result in the loss of good details.

In the last century, cleaning the family silver could take several days. In at least one house in the Berkshires, the master locked the servants in the area around the silver safe and nailed shut the windows so that no silver could be passed to anyone outside. Diligent housekeepers used whiting and water to remove tarnish, then, using a leather pad, rubbed in a combination of rouge powder and water, washed the object, and then rubbed it with dry whiting and leather. The "easy" method involved flannel, soap, and water, and a bit of soft leather to dry with. Today, the best thing to do is wash silver immediately after use. Never wash knives in the dishwasher—this harms the glue joining the blade to the handle.

Also, don't mix stainless and silver in the same wash, as pitting can occur. Use silver-polishing gloves or soft treated cloths instead of highly abrasive polishes—and keep in mind that the more you use your silver, the less tarnished it will get. Don't store your silver in plastic wrap or plastic bags; treated cloth bags and cases are best. Be sure to empty salt shakers and cellars before putting them away, as salt can damage the silver. And for heaven's sake, stop worrying! Silver is meant to be used and enjoyed, over and over again.

Table accessories can enliven any setting, especially if the piece is flamboyantly ornamented, like this champagne bucket at top left. Thematic decoration, particularly fruits of the vine, was very common on serving pieces, such as the enchanting 1860 grape tree at right.

Napkin rings were originally intended to identify and hold napkins that might be used for several meals before being washed. Large repoussé napkin rings, below left, and amusing figural napkin rings on wheels, right, are attractive and practical. This commemorative Revere bowl makes a wonderful vessel for flowers, placed on an old dish cross (a forerunner of a trivet).

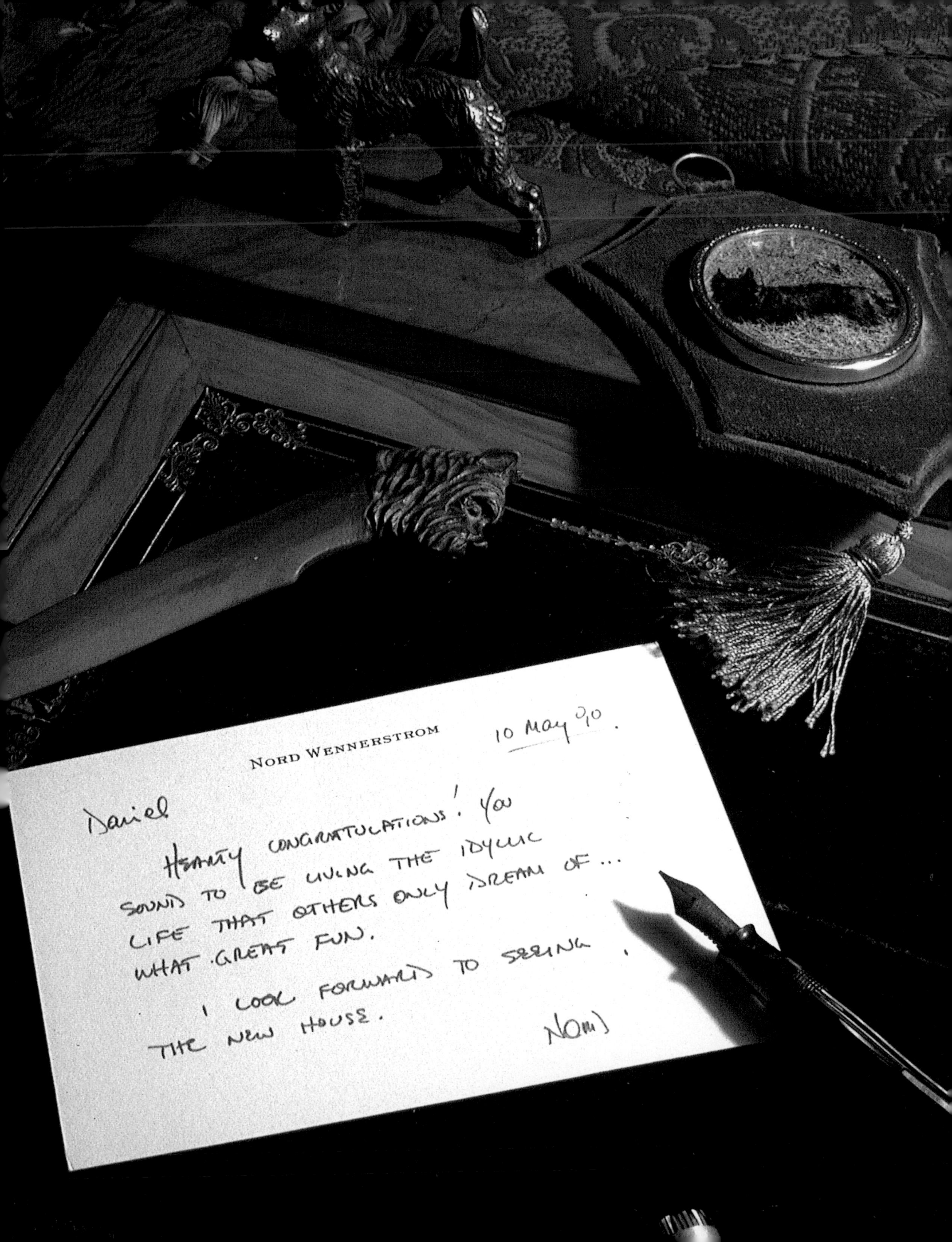
NORD WENNERSTROM
10 May 90.
Daniel
HEARTY CONGRATULATIONS! YOU
SOUND TO BE LIVING THE IDYLLIC
LIFE THAT OTHERS ONLY DREAM OF...
WHAT GREAT FUN.
I LOOK FORWARD TO SEEING
THE NEW HOUSE.
NORD

Lion's Gate at Tanglewood

ACKNOWLEDGMENTS

Once the sheer labor of writing and producing a book containing three hundred or more photographs taken on location was finished, I heaved a sigh of relief—the end, a mere list of acknowledgments, was in sight. At this point, I retrieved the myriad scraps of paper on which I'd been listing names and addresses and was stunned at their aggregate number. As I studied the photographs, I found I was reliving and mentally counting heads at each day's shoot—a necessity, since I was the crew's "mother" and provider of lunch. What suddenly dawned on me, in attempting to thank those who made this book a reality, was that it was a labor of love, not just a job, to those who brought their enthusiasm, creativity, and caring to the set each day. We lived and worked together during the late spring and one of the hottest summers in the Berkshires, becoming a team that accomplished visual miracles with efficiency and spirit. Now to say thank you . . .

First to my co-author, Joshua Greene, whose vision, talents, insights, and masterful photos brought my ideas to fruition: his creative drive and energy always brought more than the best out of us all.

To my husband, Mike Chefetz, who supported and helped all of us throughout, while playing host to a full house.

To our kids, Jill, Laurence, Andia, Alex, Eugenie, and Natasha, who good-naturedly adjusted to the chaos of the summer of '91.

To Susanna Stratton-Norris, for her keen eye and creative flair in coordinating and styling the photography, and also for being the friend, support, and motivating force that pushed me into the antiques business after a fateful visit to The Dining Room Shop in London.

To Alexandra Enders, whose words captured my thoughts and stirred my imagination, and whose enthusiasm never waned when our project was slow in getting under way.

To Susan Williams, whose historical research and knowledge of domestic life and its furnishings became the backbone of our book.

To the late Beverly Barnes, whose observations made me love silver almost as much as she did; to Pat Barrett, whose silver baskets survived the trip from Illinois to Massachusetts; and to Leon and Judith Chipkin, whose dollhouses got us started.

To Gayle Benderoff, our calm and supportive agent, who made all the right calls.

To Michael Fragnito and Barbara Williams at Viking Studio Books for their patient support of a first-time author.

To Susan Slover and her associate Sonia Biancalani-Levethan for their imaginative and meticulous eye for design.

To Joshua's crew, who did the heavy-duty work, including "Uncle Bobby" Sanchez; Karl Horner; our student helper, Emily Barnes; and especially Soffie Kage, our beautiful red-haired muse-in-residence.

Joshua would like to extend his special thanks to: Lee Bailey, whose style and simplicity have always been an inspiration; and to the "queen of country," Mary Emmerling, whose kindness has brought him involvement on many fun book projects.

For my own crew, the thanks go to . . .

Kris Allen and Mattie Kyle, who kept all my correspondence and credit straight.

A C K N O W L E D G E M E N T S

Edith Dorsett, who kept my household going.

Al Gennari, who made last-minute props.

Mariette Bertelli and Marilyn Avratin, who kept my shop, The Country Dining Room Antiques, functioning and kept track of all my borrowing.

To the incredibly talented floral designers Barbara Bockbrader, Pamela Hardcastle, and Georgene Poliak, my eternal thanks and admiration for the beauty and life their natural arrangements brought to our table "landscapes."

Food styling, a difficult and time-consuming art, was made easier by Susan Brown Draudt; David Lawson, former chef at Inn on the Green in New Marlborough, Massachusetts, who subsequently moved to Blantyre; and everyone at Special Teas in New York, Guido's Marketplace, and Day's Catch Seafood at Guido's in Pittsfield, Massachusetts. Our beautiful wedding cake was the delicious work of Cathy Taub, the former pastry chef at Blantyre, now at La Bruschetta. The Bakers Wife in Great Barrington, Massachusetts, supplied our garden tea sweets, and the Suchele Bakery in Lenox created the tasty bake-sale buffet.

The sure hand of Carole Maurer of Westport, Connecticut, is evident in the exquisite calligraphy seen throughout the photographs.

For an author to thank her insurance agents may be unusual, but the value and fragility of items borrowed for photography were such that this book could not have been done without the special efforts of Mark Selkowitz and Kim Knights of Colt Insurance in Pittsfield, Massachusetts. Because we did have coverage, we were able to obtain many beautiful and often rare objects from fine dealers in New York and the Berkshires. Their names are all listed by category in our Sources, but there are a special few to be singled out. They include Judy Egan, who suggested I call Edith Wolf Greenspan at Bardith, who in turn constantly reassured me that "It would be easy"; Marcie Imberman of Kentshire Galleries; Julie Sogg Seymour of James II; and Susan Volk of Fortunoff. Ron Hoffman of Hoffman-Gampetro, James McConnaughy of Shrubsole, and Jane Clement at Julian Graham-White are other New York City sources that were especially helpful.

In the Berkshires, David Hubregson and Douglas Howes of Aardenberg Antiques; David Good, Robert Hutchinson, Karl Lescarbeau, and Thomas Kierzek of Good and Hutchinson; Scott Sawyer; the late Marie Whitney Bonadies; the late Ambassador Graham Parsons III; and Joan Kaminow all displayed enduring patience while we photographed their wonderful home interiors. Andrea and Alan Koppel of Iris Cottage Antiques in Canaan, New York, were available day and night to fill our glass needs and offer invaluable information on the history of American pressed glass. Many individuals lent antiques that we photographed in other people's settings. They include Suzi Forbes Chase, who lent her figural napkin rings; Sally Carr Hannafin, who lent us her heirloom Wedgwood Hunt Scene dinner service; the people at Coakley Farms, who supplied hunting attire; Mona Sherman, who let us borrow her delicate fish service; Audrey Sussman, who lent her asparagus servers; Suzanne Yale, who lent us her silver candleshades; and Judy Dillenberg, who had magical cupboards filled with china and glassware treasures. Robert Herron and Lois Bradford, Berkshire-area auctioneers, also came to our rescue with some much-needed objects.

The beautiful table linens that provided the backdrop and necessary accessories for our fine table appointments came from many sources and they, too, are listed. Patrizia Anichini of Anichini Linens, however, provided most everything we needed, often at a moment's notice. She was a patient and generous lender of overwhelming amounts of the most elegant antique and contemporary table linens in a rainbow of colors.

Roseline Crowley, representing Patrick Frey, Pierre Frey, and Penelope, was another generous provider of contemporary linens. Glenn Hanna of Glenn Thomas Linens added immensely to our "Lincoln Dinner," as did Li Edelkoort with her (onion) inspiration.

We are grateful for the many doors that were opened to us by those in charge at some of the Berkshire area's historic homes. Carolyne Banfield, the Executive Director of the Berkshire County Historical Society, and Barbara Allen extended their welcome

and help at Herman Melville's Arrowhead. Thomas Hayes was an enthusiastic and genial host at The Mount. Paul Ivory and Linda Jackson made accessible the magnificent vistas and background at Chesterwood. We all have a special fondness for Naumkeag, now managed by the Trustees of Reservations under the supervision of Stanley Pratsek. The very first photographs for our book proposal were done at Naumkeag with the special help of Delphine Phelps, whose efforts smoothed the way not only at Naumkeag but at its neighboring cottage, Bonnie Brae.

We were made to feel like guests, albeit ahead of the season, at some of the Berkshires' famous hotels and inns. For this, thanks to Roderick Anderson at Blantyre, Enid Zuckerman and Art Brown at Canyon Ranch, Leslie Miller and Brad Wagstaff at Inn on the Green in New Marlborough, Massachusetts, Linfield Simon at Wheatleigh, and Margaret Kingman of Peirson Place.

Many individuals and families were kind enough to invite us into their homes, despite the natural tendency of people in this area toward low-key privacy. In many cases, they provided

keen insight into Berkshires history. Our thanks to: Herbert and Angela Abelow; Nicholas and the late Marie Whitney Bonadies; Robert and Marcia Brolli; Richard and Anne Brown; Walter and Ursula Cliff; Daniel Dempsey and Steven Rufo; John and Nancy Dinan; Hon. Jack and Jane Fitzpatrick; David Good, Robert Hutchinson, Karl Lescarbeau, and Thomas Kierzack; David Hubregsen and Douglas Howes; Margaret Kingman; Edward and Joan Kaminow; Karl and Marianne Lipsky; Juan Pablo and Pilar Molyneux; the late J. Graham Parsons III; Peggy Sawyer; Scott Sawyer; Wynn and Elizabeth Sayman; and Charles and Carole Schultze.

The Mount: Edith Wharton Restoration

GLOSSARY

ACID ETCHING
A technique for decorating silver and glass in which the surface is covered with wax except where the design is to appear. Acid is applied to the non-waxed surfaces, thus etching away the design; in glass, the results appear frosted.

AIR TWIST
A decoration in the stem of a wine glass made by drawing out and twisting an air bubble in the glass to form an intricate spiral. The technique was common from 1740 to 1770.

BONE CHINA
A white, translucent, ceramic body made from china clay and bone ash, first manufactured in England in 1748. Josiah Spode popularized the material and it became the standard English medium during the nineteenth century.

BRITANNIA METAL
A white metal (an alloy of tin, copper, and antimony, it is similar to but more malleable than pewter) used in the making of silver plate and electroplated objects during the nineteenth century.

CAMEO GLASS
Glassware that actually consists of several layers of glass, each a different color. Parts of the top layers are cut or etched away to create multi-colored designs. The outer layer, usually lighter than the inner layers, carries the design.

CASED GLASS
Also called Overlay. For cased glass, several layers of glass are engraved to reveal a different-colored layer underneath.

CASTING
A traditional technique used to create high-relief decoration in silver spouts, feet, finials, and handles. The molds were hand carved by craftsmen and then the cast parts were soldered to the raised body of the object.

CELLARETTE
A wooden box designed for storing wine, also called a *garde de vin*.

CHASING
A technique for decorating silver by indenting the metal in linear patterns with a hammer and punches.

CHINESE EXPORT PORCELAIN
Largely blue-and-white wares made in China expressly for export to the West, and often according to European tastes, from the sixteenth to nineteenth centuries. The three biggest sources were Nanking, Fitzhugh, and Canton.

CHIPPENDALE, THOMAS (1718–1779)
English furniture designer and cabinetmaker. The term Chippendale is used to describe a rococo style of the second half of the eighteenth century, characterized by ornate carving, ball-and-claw feet, and the use of Gothic and chinoiserie design elements.

COALPORT
Since 1780, an important English producer of bone china tea and dessert wares in the stylistic tradition of Sèvres and Meissen.

CREAMWARE
A pale yellow low-fired earthenware coated with a liquid lead glaze developed by Josiah Wedgwood and others during the eighteenth century.

CUT GLASS
Glass that is carved or ground down by revolving wheels to make decorative, prismatic patterns.

DELFTWARE
A tin-glazed earthenware, usually with blue and white painted decoration, produced during the eighteenth century in imitation of expensive Chinese porcelains.

DIAPER
A decorative pattern consisting of repeating geometric shapes, often diamonds and squares.

DRESDEN
An important German ceramic center, especially for large faience jars, pots, and figures, from the eighteenth century on.

EARTHENWARE
Pottery that is porous unless glazed. There are many different types of earthenwares, ranging from rough redwares to highly refined creamwares.

ELECTROPLATE
A method developed in the early nineteenth century for coating objects made of Britannia or other base metals with silver, using electric currents.

EMBOSSING
A technique for decorating silver in which the back of an object is punched to create beading—or a line of round bosses—on its front.

ENAMELING
A decorative form using vitreous pastes, often colors or gold, painted on glass, ceramic, or silver objects and then fired to create colorful patterns.

ENGINE TURNING
A mechanical process for engraving a geometric pattern into a piece of silver. The object is held in a device that moves it in a controlled pattern against a stationary engraving tool to produce a series of straight or wavy lines.

ENGRAVING
A decorative technique in which material is removed from the surface of glass or silver with a graver, a diamond-shaped steel rod.

EPERGNE
An elaborate centerpiece, often with a tall central trumpet-shaped vase form surrounded by several other vases or plates projecting at different heights from the central stem.

FAIENCE
Tin-glazed, colorfully decorated earthenware commonly produced in France.

FEDERAL
Period in American furniture from 1790–1815, characterized by neoclassical designs based on the work of English furniture designers like Thomas Sheraton and George Hepplewhite.

FLASHED
A term describing the outermost layer in glass, painted to look like cased glass.

FLINT GLASS
Originally, glass produced from powdered flint, but now also used to describe any lead glass.

FLUTING
Closely spaced concave vertical grooves.

FREE-BLOWN GLASS
Glassware that is made by blowing and shaping a bubble of molten glass into the desired shape.

GADROONING
An applied edging of closely spaced convex vertical grooves (inverted fluting).

GILDING
A coating of gold over silver objects. The most common method was mercury gilding, in which a mixture of gold and mercury was applied to silver as a paste. Upon heating, the mercury vaporized and the gold remained.

GIRANDOLE
An ornamental branched candleholder, usually brass, with hanging cut-glass prisms, flanked by a pair of candlesticks.

HALLMARKS
A variety of identification marks on silver that denote date, maker, town, fineness, and duty.

HARD PASTE PORCELAIN
"True" porcelain—hard, white, and durable—made from china stone (petuntse) and china clay (kaolin).

HAVILAND-LIMOGES
A kind of fine porcelain tableware, often made for the American market. Charles Haviland's factory in Limoges, France, was founded in the late nineteenth century.

HEPPLEWHITE, GEORGE (D. 1786)
English cabinetmaker and furniture designer, most associated with shield- and oval-backed chairs.

HOLLOWWARE
Any three-dimensional silver object meant to contain food and/or beverages.

IMARI
Japanese porcelain made for export and characterized by bright floral or scenic patterns in blue, red, and gold.

IRONSTONE
A hard, white, nontranslucent earthenware, patented in England in 1813 by George and Charles Mason.

JASPERWARE
A vitrified earthenware invented by Josiah Wedgwood, usually with light figures in relief on a darker background.

LACY GLASS
Early pressed glass characterized by a stippled surface and intricate patterning that resembles lace.

LEAD GLASS
Glass made from lead oxide, which produces extra brilliance and resilience, often referred to as lead crystal.

LUSTER
A metallic decoration imitative of silver, copper, or gold. A thin film of gold luster applied to a brown-bodied ware produced copper luster, while gold luster applied to a white body resulted in pink. Platinum imparted a silvery surface and was often used to produce faux silver tea sets.

MAJOLICA
A highly sculptural, glazed, and richly ornamented earthenware.

MEISSEN
First porcelain manufacturers in Europe, founded in 1710 by Augustus the Strong at Meissen, near Dresden. A major force in the ceramics world thereafter, Meissen is renowned for figures and enamel painting.

MILK GLASS
Glass made with tin oxide, which produces a white, porcelain-like opacity.

MINTON
A major Staffordshire pottery founded in 1796 by Thomas Minton at Stoke-on-Trent, producing very fine earthenwares and bone china wares.

MOCHAWARE
Early nineteenth-century earthenware decorated to resemble mocha stone, a variety of quartz often streaked with fossil ferns and mosses.

MOLD-BLOWN GLASS
Glassware that is made by blowing molten glass into full-size molds that both form and decorate the object.

OVERGLAZE
Enamels, derived from metallic oxides, used to paint flowers, scenes, or other multi-colored embellishments on ceramic wares that had first been glazed and fired. The objects were then fired again, at a lower heat, to vitrify (make glasslike) the enamels.

OXIDATION
A process in which a layer of silver sulfide (tarnish) is applied to a polished silver object to achieve decorative areas of contrast.

PEARLWARE
A whiter form of creamware developed by Wedgwood in the 1770s and most often used in transfer-printed wares.

PETUNTSE
China stone, a partially decomposed form of granite, used in making porcelain.

PLANISHING
A silver smoothing process in which the surface of an object was hammered with the convex head of a planishing hammer. The piece was then filed to remove any marks, rubbed with pumice, polished with a smooth stone, and buffed; in the late nineteenth century, planishing marks were intentionally left on or artificially created to suggest handwork.

POLYCHROME
Multi-colored.

PONTIL
A tool used in free blown glassmaking to remove the glass object from the blow pipe; the mark left on the object after removal is called the punty or the pontil mark.

PORCELAIN
A ceramic substance made of kaolin and petuntse, fired at high temperature to produce fine, hard, white, impermeable wares. First made in China between the seventh and eighth centuries.

PRESSED GLASS
Glassware that is made by mechanically pressing molten glass into molds.

RAISING
A process, used for creating deep silver vessels, in which a silver disk was crimped or shaped over a raising stake and hammered into the desired shape.

REDWARE
Earthenware made from clays containing iron.

REGENCY
An English term for neoclassical objects made during the first forty years of the nineteenth century; specifically, the term refers to the Regency of George, Prince of Wales (1811–1820).

REPOUSSÉ
French for "pushed out," a form of high relief chasing, done from inside a silver vessel. The design is first chased on the outside, then the chased areas are hammered out into dimensional shape and size from the inside with a snarling iron.

SALT GLAZE
A hard, shiny, textured, transparent glaze on pottery achieved by throwing salt into the kiln during the firing process.

SATIN GLASS
A type of art glass with a lusterless, soft-looking surface, achieved by acid etching or sandblasting.

SCRATCH BLUE
Incised designs in stoneware filled with blue cobalt, typical of eighteenth-century salt-glazed stoneware.

SEVRES
France's Royal Porcelain Factory, and Europe's foremost porcelain manufacturer, founded in 1738 in Vincennes but moved to Sèvres in the mid-1700s.

SHEFFIELD PLATE
An early form of silver plate in which a thin bar of silver was fused to a much thicker bar of copper (on both sides if necessary). The procedure began in Sheffield, England, in the 1760s.

SHERATON, THOMAS (1751–1806)
English furniture designer, best known for elegant styles characterized by straight lines, graceful proportions, and satinwood inlays.

SILVER PLATE
A thin layer of silver that coats metal objects.

SINKING
A process used for creating shallow silver vessels in which a disk, taken from a sheet of silver, was hammered into a concave wooden form by a silversmith.

SLIP
Clay thinned with water and used to glaze or paint designs on ceramics.

SOFT PASTE PORCELAIN
"Imitation" porcelain—a combination of white clay and ground glass, fired at a lower temperature than true porcelain, then lead glazed and decorated with enamels.

SPATTERWARE
Inexpensive nineteenth-century pottery decorated with a "spattered" pattern.

SPODE
English pottery famous for creamwares, pearlwares, bone china, and stone china, founded around 1770 by Josiah Spode.

SPONGEWARE
Inexpensive nineteenth-century pottery decorated with a sponge soaked in slip, which was then applied to the object's surface.

STAFFORDSHIRE
Center of English ceramic production, renowned for producing both porcelains and earthenwares.

STERLING
The standard of fineness, established in the twelfth century, given to silver: .925 part silver to .75 part copper or other base metal.

STONE CHINA
Stoneware made with china stone (petuntse), developed in the early nineteenth century by Spode.

STONEWARE
A high-fired ceramic body, harder than earthenware, not as fine as porcelain, most commonly coarse gray in color.

TASTE-VIN
A small, flat silver bowl used for wine tasting.

TAZZA
A wide shallow bowl set on a stem.

TRANSFERWARE
Ceramics decorated by transfer printing. A copper plate, engraved with a design, was inked with colored glaze and printed onto tissue (the bat); the tissue was then burnished onto the object to be decorated, soaked off, fired to affix the design, and glazed.

TREEN
Small wooden objects made for domestic purposes.

UNDERGLAZE
Printed or painted decoration, most commonly a layer of cobalt oxide, applied to ceramic objects before the final glazing process. Underglazing was practiced by Chinese potters in the fourteenth century, migrated west, and, by the late eighteenth century, was used on stoneware, delftware, pearlware, and porcelain.

Naumkeag

BIBLIOGRAPHY

Andrews, Julia C. Breakfast, Dinner and Tea. New York: D. W. Appleton and Company, 1869.

Aslet, Clive. The American Country House. New Haven: Yale University Press, 1990.

Banister, Judith, ed. English Silver Hallmarks. Des Moines, Iowa: Wallace-Homestead Book Co., 1970.

Barry, Roxana. Land of Plenty: 19th Century American Picnic and Harvest Scenes. New York: The Katonah Gallery,

Beeton, Isabella. Beeton's Book of Household Management 1859–1861. (Facsimile ed.) London: Chancellor Press, 1982.

Belden, Louise Conway. Marks of American Silversmiths. Charlottesville: University Press of Virginia, 1980.

Carter, Mary E. Millionaire Households. New York: D. Appleton and Company, 1903.

Chippendale, Thomas. The Gentleman & Cabinet-maker's Director. (Reprint of 3rd ed., 1762.) New York: Dover Publications, 1966.

Davidson, Marshall B., and Elizabeth Stillinger. The American Wing at the Metropolitan Museum of Art. New York: Alfred A. Knopf, 1985.

Eastlake, Charles Locke. Hints on Household Taste in Furniture, Upholstery, and Other Details. Boston: J. R. Osgood and Company, 1872.

Ellet, Elizabeth, ed. The New Cyclopaedia of Domestic Economy, and Practical Housekeeper. Norwich, Conn.: Henry Bill Publishing Co., 1873.

Farrar, Mrs. John. The Young Lady's Friend. Boston: American Stationer's Co., 1836.

Garrett, Elisabeth Donaghy. At Home: The American Family 1750–1870. New York: Harry N. Abrams, Inc., 1989.

Girouard, Mark. The Victorian Country House. New Haven: Yale University Press, 1979.

Godden, Geoffrey. Encyclopedia of British Pottery and Porcelain Marks. Exton, Pa.: Schiffler Publishing, Ltd., 1964.

Green, Harvey. The Light of the Home: An Intimate View of the Lives of Women in Victorian America. New York: Pantheon Books, 1983.

Grover, Katherine, ed. Dining in America, 1850–1900. Amherst: The University of Massachusetts Press, and Rochester, N.Y.: The Margaret Woodbury Strong Museum, 1987.

Harland, Marion. Breakfast, Luncheon and Tea. New York: Charles Scribner's Sons, 1875.

Hepplewhite, George. The Cabinet-maker and Upholsterer's Guide. (Reprint of 3rd ed., 1794.) New York: Dover Publications, 1969.

Hodgson, Mrs. Willoughby. How to Identify Old China. London: G. Bell and Sons, 1904.

Hughes, G. Bernard. Antique Sheffield Plate. London: B. T. Batsford Ltd., 1970.

————. Small Antique Silverware. New York: Bramhall House, 1957.

Kovel, Ralph and Terry. New Dictionary of Marks. New York: Crown Publishers, 1986.

Latham, Jean. The Pleasure of Your Company: A History of Manners and Morals. London: A. and C. Black, 1972.

Lewis, R. W. B. and Nancy. The Letters of Edith Wharton. New York: Collier Books, 1988.

Lichten, Frances. Decorative Art of Victoria's Era. New York: Charles Scribner's Sons, 1950.

Livesy, Anthony. A Treasury of World Antiques. New York: The Hamlyn Publishing Group and Crescent Books, 1979.

Loftie, M. J. The Dining Room. New York: Garland Publishers, 1878, 1978.

Morton, Agnes. Etiquette. Philadelphia: Pennsylvania Publishing Co., 1894.

Ohrbach, Barbara Milo. Antiques at Home. New York: Clarkson N. Potter, Inc., 1989.

Oliver, Raymond. The French at Table. London: The Wine and Food Society, 1967.

Osterberg, Richard F., and Betty Smity. Silver Flatware Dictionary. San Diego: A. S. Barnes, 1981.

Owens, Carole. The Berkshire Cottages, A Vanishing Era. Englewood Cliffs, N.J.: Cottage Press, Inc. 1984.

Phillips, Phoebe, ed. The Collectors' Encyclopedia of Antiques. New York: Bonanza Books, 1973.

————. The Encyclopedia of Glass. New York: Crown Publishers, 1981.

Powers, Lyall H. Henry James and Edith Wharton: Letters: 1900–1915. New York: Charles Scribner's Sons, 1990.

Praz, Mario. An Illustrated History of Interior Decoration from Pompeii to Art Nouveau. London: Thames and Hudson, 1983.

Sandwith, Hermione, and Sheila Stainton. The National Trust Manual of Housekeeping. London: Penguin Books, 1986.

Sheraton, Thomas. The Cabinet-maker and Upholsterer's Drawing-Book. (Reprint of 1793 ed.) New York: Dover Publications, 1972.

Sprackling, Helen. Customs of the Table Top: How New England Housewives Set Out Their Tables. Sturbridge, Mass.: Old Sturbridge Village, 1958.

Tannahill, Reay. Food in History. New York: Crown, 1988.

Wharton, Edith. The Custom of the Country. New York: Bantam Books, 1991.

———. The House of Mirth. New York: W. W. Norton & Co., 1990.

———, and Ogden Codman. The Decoration of Houses. (Reprint of 1897 ed.) New York: W. W. Norton, 1978.

Williams, Susan. Savory Suppers and Fashionable Feasts: Dining in America. New York: Pantheon Books, 1985.

Wolfe, Linda. The Literary Gourmet: Menus from Masterpieces. New York: Harmony Books, 1985.

SOURCES

ANTIQUES

AARDENBURG INN AND ANTIQUES
144 West Pike
Lee, MA 01238
413-243-0001
Fine furniture, porcelains.
Pages 127, 203

AARON'S ANTIQUES
Manhattan Antique Center
1050 Second Avenue
New York, NY 10022
212-644-5868
Silver.
Page 49

A.D.C. HERITAGE
485 Park Avenue
New York, NY 10022
212-750-2664
English silver.
Pages 36, 80, 192

BARDITH LTD.
901 Madison Avenue
New York, NY 10021
212-737-3775
English china and glass.
Pages 15, 21, 23, 34, 36, 46, 69, 75, 142, 143, 158, 205

PATRICK BARRETT
140 German Church Road
Hinsdale, IL 60521
708-887-1043
Silver.
Page 197

BRADFORD GALLERIES, LTD.
Route 7
Sheffield, MA 01257
413-229-6667
Rugs, silver.

CDR SHADE COMPANY
178 Main Street
Great Barrington, MA 01230
413-528-5050
Candleshades.
Pages 17, 38, 40, 45, 80, 81

CORASHIRE ANTIQUES
Belcher Square
Great Barrington, MA 01230
413-528-0014
American country furniture.
Pages 136, 138, 139

CORNER HOUSE ANTIQUES
Route 7
Sheffield, MA 01257
413-229-6627
Wicker furniture.
Pages 24, 26, 27

THE COUNTRY DINING ROOM ANTIQUES
178 Main Street
Great Barrington, MA 01230
413-528-5050
China, silver, glass, furniture.
Pages 6, 9, 10, 20, 28, 38, 40, 45, 49, 57, 67, 73, 91, 95, 97, 123, 153, 161, 162, 163, 182, 183, 185, 186, 198

FORTUNOFF
681 Fifth Avenue
New York, NY 10022
212-758-6660
Silver.
Pages 75, 79, 85, 115, 143, 195, 200, 206, 211, 213

BERNICE FRIED
Manhattan Antique Center
1050 Second Avenue
New York, NY 10022
212-751-1860
Silver salt.
Page 204

JAMIE GIBBS INTERIORS
340 East 93rd Street
New York, NY 10028
212-722-7508
Candelabra.
Page 87

GOOD & HUTCHINSON & ASSOCIATES
Route 7
Sheffield, MA 01257
413-229-8832
Furniture, china, silver.
Pages 47, 92, 93, 132, 156

GORHAM INC.
P. O. Box 6150
Providence, RI 02940
401-333-4360
Silver.
Pages 25, 88, 191

ROBERT HERRON AUCTIONS
Route 22
Austerlitz, NY 12017
518-392-5478
Furniture, rugs.
Pages 69, 104

HOFFMAN & GAMPETRO ANTIQUES
Manhattan Antique Center
1050 Second Avenue
New York, NY 10022
212-755-1120
China, silver, glass.
Pages 29, 52, 65, 66, 104, 115, 158, 181, 198, 199, 208, 209

IRIS COTTAGE ANTIQUES
Route 295
Canaan, NY 12029
518-781-4379
American pressed glass.
Pages 39, 97, 176, 178, 187, 188

JAMES II
GALLERIES
15 East 57th Street
New York, NY 10022
212-355-7040
China, silver, glass, treen.
Pages 24, 72, 87, 88, 123, 204, jacket

JOAN KAMINOW
INTERIORS
Route 23, Box 162
88 Middle Road
Sands Point, NY 11050
516-944-9669
China, glass, furniture.
Pages 26, 27

KENTSHIRE
GALLERIES, LTD.
37 East 12th Street
New York, NY 10003
212-673-6644
Furniture, pottery, china, silver, glass.
Pages 9, 10, 52, 53, 76, 77, 133, 157, 185, 210

ALICE KWARTLER
ANTIQUES
Place Des Antiquaires
123 E. 57th Street/Gallery 26
New York, NY 10022
212-752-3590
Glass, silver.
Pages 87, 88, 138

MCGRORY
ANTIQUE RUGS
Castle Street
Great Barrington, MA 01230
413-528-9594
Page 87

GEORGE H. MEYER
100 West Long Lake Road
Suite 100
Bloomfield Hills, MI 48304
313-647-5111
American folk art canes.
Page 70

JUAN PABLO
MOLYNEUX STUDIO
29 East 69th Street
New York, NY 10021
212-628-0097
Pages 36, 37, 113

REED & BARTON CO.
41 Madison Avenue
New York, NY 10010
212-689-2490
Silver.
Pages 193, 194, 201

JAMES ROBINSON
480 Park Avenue
New York, NY 10022
212-752-6166
Silver.
Pages 15, 16, 73, 205

SAWYER'S ANTIQUES
Depot
West Stockbridge, MA 01266
413-232-7062
China, glass, furniture, silver.
Pages 75, 111, 155

WYNN A. SAYMAN
"Old Fields"
Richmond, MA 01254
413-698-2272
English pottery, porcelains.
Pages 144, 147, 148, 149, 159

DAVID SEIDENBERG
ANTIQUES
836 Broadway
New York, NY 10003
212-260-2810
Porcelains, glass.
Pages 32, 174, 175, 197

S.J. SHRUBSOLE
CORP.
104 East 57th Street
New York, NY 10022
212-753-8920
English silver.
Pages 34, 71, 79, 104, 205, 209

TIFFANY & CO.
727 Fifth Avenue
New York, NY 10022
212-755-8000
Silver.
Pages 9, 26, 31, 53, 74

TUDOR ROSE
ANTIQUES
28 East 10th Street
New York, NY 10003
212-677-5239
Silver.

MARIE WHITNEY
ANTIQUES
H.C. 68 Box 148
Tolland, MA 01034
413-258-4538
Furniture, silver, glass, china.
Pages 145, 170, 171, 172, 173, 176

S. WYLER, INC.
941 Lexington Avenue
New York, NY 10021
212-879-9848
Silver.
Pages 29, 212, jacket

LINENS

ANICHINI LINENS
745 Fifth Avenue, Suite 2007
New York, NY 10151
212-752-2130
Page 7, 9, 13, 40, 43, 46, 57, 69, 73, 75, 78, 79, 81, 94, 103, 104, 135, 163, 169, 188, 204, 205

LA SERVIETTE
1 Gracie Square
New York, NY 10028
212-288-6073
Pages 36, 204

LERON
750 Madison Avenue
New York, NY 10021
212-249-3188
Pages 19, 80, 63

PATRICK FREY
225 Fifth Avenue
New York, NY 10010
212-213-4110
Pages 25, 26, 46, 96, 98, 205

**JANA STARR/JEAN
HOFFMAN ANTIQUES**
236 East 80th Street
New York, NY 10021
212-861-8256
Pages 87, 104

**SYBARITIC
INDUSTRIES**
115 Thompkin Avenue
Pleasantville, NY 10570
914-769-7888
Page 82

GLENN THOMAS, INC.
561 Acorn Street
Deer Park, NY 11729
516-243-3330
Pages 44, 45

FLOWERS

BARBARA BOCKBRADER
Route 71
North Egremont, MA 01252
413-528-9180
Pages 17, 18, 19, 23, 24, 29, 31, 32, 34,
35, 36, 43, 53, 61, 71, 73, 75, 85, 87, 91,
96, 100, 102, 116, 131, 132, 166, 197

**PAMELA READ
HARDCASTLE**
Route 57
New Marlborough, MA 01230
413-229-8812
Pages 9,10,40,46, 47, 92, 94, 95, 110, 132

GEORGENE POLIAK
P. O. Box 393
Great Barrington, MA 01230
413-528-5263
Pages 44, 45

FOOD

THE BAKERS WIFE
312 Main Street
Great Barrington, MA 01230
413-528-4623
Page 96

**DAY'S CATCH
SEAFOOD AT GUIDO"S**
Route 7, 1020 South Street
Pittsfield, MA 01201
413-499-3619
Pages 17, 23, 24, 158

SUSAN BROWN DRAUDT
101 Colt Road
Pittsfield, MA 01201
413-443-7119
Food stylist.
Pages 31, 74, cover

**GUIDO'S
MARKETPLACE**
Route 7, 1020 South Street
Pittsfield, MA 01201
413-442-9909
Pages 17, 23, 24

DAVID LAWSON
Blantyre, Rte 20,
Lenox, MA 01240
413-637-3556
Pages 44, 45

SUCHELE BAKERS
31 Housatonic Street
Lenox, MA 01240
413-637-0939
Pages 96, 97

CATHY TAUB
La Bruschetta
Stockbridge, MA
413-232-7141
Page 85

HOTELS AND INNS

BLANTYRE
P. O. Box 995
Route 20
Lenox, MA 01240
413-637-3556

**CANYON RANCH
IN LENOX**
91 Kemble
Lenox, MA 01240
413-637-4100

INN ON THE GREEN
Route 57
New Marlborough, MA 01230
413-229-7924

THE PEIRSON PLACE
Route 41
Richmond, MA 01254
413-698-2802

RED LION INN
Main Street
Stockbridge, MA 01262
413-298-5545

WHEATLEIGH
West Hawthorne
Lenox, MA 01240
413-637-0610

Before I owned an antiques shop, I had the time, curiosity, and desire to see, do, and experience all that I could of the abundance of cultural events and natural beauties the Berkshires has to offer. It was my pleasure to do the advance scouting for family and friends who visited, to become their tour guide in person or on paper. But there is no lack of handy and useful guidebooks to be found at information booths in each town. I have found the best to be *Discover the Berkshires*, from which much of the following information was taken.

HISTORICAL SITES AND GARDENS

ARROWHEAD

Headquarters of the Berkshire County Historical Society. Built in 1780, this structure was the nineteenth-century home of author Herman Melville, who wrote *Moby Dick* and other great works here. Activities include house tours, a nature trail, a film on Berkshire history, and a gift shop.

780 Holmes Road, Pittsfield, Massachusetts
(413) 442-1793

BARTHOLEMEW'S COBBLE

More than 700 species of plants, including 40 species of ferns and many wildflowers. Activities include picnicking, bird watching, six miles of hiking trails, and a museum. Admission.
Ashley Falls, Massachusetts
(413) 229-8600

BERKSHIRE BOTANICAL GARDEN

Fifteen acres provide visitors with a place of beauty and gardeners with inspiration and information. There are intimate landscaped gardens, a terraced herb garden, a rose garden, ponds, and a woodland walk. Picnics welcome. Admission.
Routes 102 & 183, Stockbridge, Massachusetts
(413) 298-3926

BERKSHIRE SCENIC RAILWAY MUSEUM

Free Railroad Museum at historic Lenox Station. Scenic train ride along the Housatonic River.
Willow Creek Road, east end of Housatonic St., Lenox, Massachusetts
(Mailing address: P.O. Box 2195)
(413) 637-2210

THE BIDWELL HOUSE

Elegantly restored 1750 manse on National Register with superb collection of period furnishings. Admission.
Art School Road, Monterey, Massachusetts
(Mailing address: P.O. Box 537)
(413) 528-6888

WILLIAM CULLEN BRYANT HOMESTEAD

Home of the poet in his early years and later life. Period furnishings and memorabilia, with superb views. Off Route 112, Cummington, Massachusetts
(413) 634-2244

CHAPIN LIBRARY OF RARE BOOKS

Permanent displays of original printings of the Declaration of Independence, the Articles of Confederation, the Constitution, and the Bill of Rights. Thirty-thousand books and manuscripts from the nineteenth and twentieth centuries. Free.

Stetson Hall, Williams College, Williamstown, Massachusetts
(413) 597-2462

CHESTERWOOD

Summer estate of Daniel Chester French, sculptor of the "Minute Man" and the Lincoln Memorial. Studio, mansion, museum, country garden, woodland walk, plus guided tours, gift shop, and special exhibits. Admission.
Off Route 183, Glendale, Massachusetts
(413) 298-3579

COLONEL ASHLEY HOUSE

Oldest house in the Berkshires, built in 1735. Features early American furnishings, pottery collection, original wood paneling, and an herb garden. Admission.
Ashley Falls, Massachusetts
(413) 298-3239

CRANE MUSEUM

Historical exhibits of fine papermaking systems since 1801, including those used in the printing of U.S. currency. Free.
Off Route 9, Dalton, Massachusetts
(413) 684-2600

HANCOCK SHAKER VILLAGE

Restored Shaker Community (1790–1960)—and living, working museum of rural Shaker life in 20 buildings on 1,200 acres. Activities include Shaker music programs, nineteenth-century crafts demonstrations and workshops, plus exhibits, herb and vegetable gardens, farm animals, special events, and, from July–October, special candlelight Shaker dinners. Gift shops feature reproduction Shaker furniture and crafts produced at the Village.
Route 20, five miles west of Pittsfield, Massachusetts
(413) 443-0188

THE MOUNT

Pulitzer prize-winning author Edith Wharton built The Mount in 1902 on the classical precepts of her popular book *The Decoration of Houses* (1897). Admission.

Plunkett St., Lenox, Massachusetts

(413) 637-1899

MT. GREYLOCK VISITORS CENTER

Environmental displays, trail maps, and information.

Off Route 7, Mt. Greylock, Massachusetts

(413) 499-4262

MT. LEBANON SHAKER VILLAGE

Self-guided outdoor walking tours of 25 original buildings. Permanent and revolving exhibits at 1854 Wash House and 1829 Brethren's Workshop. Route 20, nine miles west of Pittsfield at Darrow School, Mt. Lebanon, New York. (Mailing address: P.O. Box 628)

(518) 794-9500

MISSION HOUSE

House, furnishings, and garden are excellent examples of Colonial architecture and style. Also contains newly renovated Indian museum. Admission.

West Main St., Stockbridge, Massachusetts

(413) 298-3239

NAUMKEAG

Designed by Stanford White and built in 1886 for Joseph Choate, Ambassador to England. Features include original furnishings, formal gardens with promenades, fountains, and terraces. Guided house tours. Admission.

Prospect Hill Rd., Stockbridge, Massachusetts

(413) 298-3239

ALBERT SCHWEITZER CENTER

Museum, library, and archival collection containing photographs, films, tapes, and memorabilia about Dr. Schweitzer. Children's garden and wildlife sanctuary. Donation.

Hurlburt Road, Great Barrington, Massachusetts

(413) 528-3124

ART MUSEUMS

THE BERKSHIRE MUSEUM

Berkshire County's museum of art, history, and natural history. Strong collection of Hudson River School landscapes. Exhibits of animals and birds, biology, and minerals. Fresh and salt water aquarium. Museum shop. Admission.

39 South Street, Pittsfield, Massachusetts

(413) 443-7171

STERLING AND FRANCINE CLARK ART INSTITUTE

Important nineteenth-century paintings by Corot, Renoir, Degas, Monet, Toulouse-Lautrec, Winslow Homer. Old Master paintings, prints and drawings; sculpture by Degas; English and American silver. Special exhibits, guided tours.

225 South St., Williamstown, Massachusetts

(413) 458-9545

NORMAN ROCKWELL MUSEUM

The largest collection in the world of original art by America's favorite illustrator. Admission.

Main St., Stockbridge, Massachusetts

(413) 298-3822 or 298-3944

WILLIAMS COLLEGE MUSEUM OF ART

Contemporary and modern art, American art from the eighteenth century to the present, and non-Western art. Active program of special exhibits presents outstanding works from other collections. Free.

Main St. (Route 2), Williamstown, Massachusetts

(413) 597-2429